ALSO BY AARON KARO

Ruminations on College Life

RUMINATIONS

on

TWENTY
SOMETHING

life

AARON KARO

A Fireside Book
Published by Simon & Schuster
New York   London   Toronto   Sydney

FIRESIDE
Rockefeller Center
1230 Avenue of the Americas
New York, NY 10020

FIRESIDE and colophon are registered trademarks
of Simon & Schuster, Inc.

Portions of this book originally appeared in the
email column "RUMINATIONS."

For information about special discounts for bulk purchases,
please contact Simon & Schuster Special Sales at
1-800-456-6798 or business@simonandschuster.com

Designed by William Ruoto

Manufactured in the United States of America

10   9   8   7   6   5   4   3   2   1

Library of Congress Cataloging-in-Publication Data
Karo, Aaron.
Ruminations on twenty something life / Aaron Karo.
                                         p.   cm.
                              "A Fireside book."
1. Youth—Humor. 2. Young adults—Humor. I. Title.
                          PN6231.A26K37 2005
          818'.5402—dc22   2004058624

ISBN 0-7432-6963-2

For Brian

Friend, Roommate, Partner in Crime.

By the way, you owe me twenty bucks. Dick.

ACKNOWLEDGMENTS

I would like to thank . . .

My parents—for cutting me off financially immediately after I graduated from college, thereby forcing me to write books to make ends meet. You always said I could move back home if necessary but silently prayed it would never happen. Also for your unwavering love and support, which thankfully is still free of charge.

My sister, Caryn—for keeping me on my toes. A few years after I went away to school, you went away to school. A few years after I graduated, you graduated. Even though you're a copycat, I still love you. You once said you looked up to me, but really it's me who looks up to you.

My friends—for continuously providing me with fodder to repackage and sell to the masses. Please keep getting drunk, falling down, and saying stupid things. I live for that. Those who know me best know I only make fun of those I care about. And after reading this book you'll know I must really, really care about you.

ESPN.com—for your up-to-the-minute scores and insightful reporting. I visited you every two minutes while writing this book and you never ceased to amaze me.

A.B. Fischer, Darren Trattner, and Allyson Peltier—for getting me another book deal. You guys did good. Of course, I wrote my last book for fifty bucks and a pretzel keg, so it was hard to do worse. Still, your tireless work is greatly appreciated.

My editor, Sara Schapiro—for finally allowing me to use dirty language in a book. Also for putting up with me when I refused to use any semicolons or the word "whom," because I think they're weird. Finally, for your unending patience and guidance. When your red pen consigned one of my jokes to oblivion, it was with infinite tenderness.

Twentysomethings everywhere—for owning the toilets and coffee tables on top of which this book will surely rest. Your trials and tribulations inspired me to chronicle my own. Your job sucks. Your apartment sucks. You're not getting laid. But at least we have each other. This book is for you. Because we could all use a good laugh.

CONTENTS

RUMINATIONS
on
TWENTY
SOMETHING
life

INTRODUCTION
welcome to twentysomething life

In a nutshell, being twentysomething means you are only concerned with two things: trying to get laid and trying not to get laid off. It also means that, for a while, birthdays become much less important. Shortly after I turned twenty-four, I realized what a meaningless milestone it was. After all, turning nineteen is a big deal because it's your last year as a teenager and your twentieth birthday is important because it's the beginning of your twenties. And at twenty-one, you are, at long last, legal. But from twenty-two to twenty-four, not much happens. Once you get past your "I wish I was still in college phase," you sort of get into a groove for a few years and refuse to look ahead. Then all of a sudden your twenty-fifth birthday comes along and all hell breaks loose. Next thing you know you're engaged and living in the suburbs spending your weekends at Crate & Barrel shopping for placemats. But before you hit the big Two-Five, your early twenties can be some of the most carefree and amazing years of your life. In fact, if your adolescence can be described as the "Wonder Years," then I say that ages twenty-two, twenty-three, and twenty-four deserve to get their own name too—the "Whatever Years."

But before I take you on this journey through my Whatever Years, I must first take you back to where it all began. In September 1997, as a hard-partying freshman at the University of Pennsylvania, I began writing emails filled with anecdotes and observations about college life to twenty of my high school buddies. By the time I graduated four years later, those emails had spawned a regular column with over 11,000 subscribers around the world. Within a year, I had published *Ruminations on College Life,* a compilation of those emails, and began a new column called "RUMINATIONS." The new column picked up where the book left off, detailing my evolution from frat boy to manhood and following my adventures as a single twentysomething in New York City. By the time I reached my twenty-fifth birthday in the summer of 2004, I had nearly 40,000 subscribers worldwide, all stemming from those twenty friends from high school. This book is a compilation of the best of "RUMINATIONS" as well as brand-new, previously unpublished material.

At the end of *Ruminations on College Life,* I asked the question, "Is there life after college?" This book is my answer. The Whatever Years officially begin upon graduation, which is a strange and unique time because you are all of a sudden living in the gap between college and marriage, between zero responsibility and total responsibility. A lot of people start freaking out. But I'll help you get through it. Each chapter in this book represents a different facet of twentysomething life as seen through the eyes of a recovering frat boy. But bear in mind, nowhere in this book will you find any practical advice. You won't learn to cook or find a job or get a date. Why? Because I have no idea how to do those things either. What you will learn is that you are not alone, that your early twenties are surprisingly like mine, and that there's no reason to start freaking out—you'll figure everything out as you go along. So whether you're twentysomething now, fondly looking back at your Whatever Years, or warily looking ahead to them, I hope you will read my book and laugh out loud. Is there life after college? Hell yeah, and there's not a placemat in sight.

ONE

the roommate

I was lucky enough to have had a single all four years of college, so I'd never really lived with anyone until I moved to Manhattan. After graduating from Penn, I decided to live with my buddy Brian, who had just graduated from Cornell. We'd been friends for fifteen years and grew up only a few blocks away from each other on Long Island. Brian and I were close friends and I knew he was quirky. For instance, he once claimed he could tell the difference between 1% and 2% milk just on sight. (He actually can.) Still, you don't really get to know someone until you live with them for years separated only by a three-inch temporary plaster wall.

As soon as Brian and I moved into our apartment, I noticed that the roommate relationship is very different if the roommates are guys than if they're girls. If Brian didn't come home one night, I thought to myself, all right, he must be getting some ass! But if a girl's roommate doesn't come home in time for *Sex and the City,* she calls the police. If you're a guy and your roommate doesn't come home for two days, instead of being more worried, you're more excited and think to yourself, damn, he must be getting some *serious* ass!

Brian and I have spent a lot of time together over the past few years. Probably because bad things happen when we're apart. When I was in the hospital for a few days with appendicitis, he threw a party and almost got us thrown out of the apartment. And once when Brian returned from a weeklong vacation, we almost came to blows when he tried to get me to itemize the air conditioning bill for the time he was gone. But while we might squabble over money and toilet paper, Brian and I are always friends in the end. We have no choice—both of our names are on the lease.

BRIAN IS A meal-describer. Meaning that when he comes home from dinner, I get a detailed, play-by-play account of everything he ate: "Karo, you should have seen this sandwich I had, man. It came on a semolina roll with the mozzarella melted just right. The chicken was topped with red onions, bell peppers, and—" I'm like, "Dude, will you shut the fuck up, I'm trying to watch *Family Guy*." Of course, my efforts are in vain, because Brian is a connoisseur of all things culinary. He once almost got into a fistfight with his girlfriend's parents during a friendly game of Scattergories because he insisted olive loaf was a food that started with the letter *O*. And after inspecting a new gourmet bakery that opened up down the block, he stormed out declaring he would never return. When I asked him why, he said, "They can't fool me, those are store-bought croutons, I can tell by the texture." Brian loves family-style restaurants, pours the salt onto his hand and then onto his food because he says it gives him "better control," and, appropriately enough, his plate-cleaning abilities put mine to shame.

BRIAN REDEFINES "thinking with your stomach." He actually remembers dates by recalling what food he ate that day. I once asked him if he knew when he last paid the cable bill. He thought for a moment and then said, "It was eleven days ago on a Tuesday. I remember because I had this amazing porterhouse the night before." Brian once fell asleep in bed with a half-eaten grilled chicken sandwich in his hand, once claimed to have a "meat hangover" after dining at an all-you-can-eat Brazilian restaurant, and once spent half an hour debating with his friend whether a 14-inch pizza referred to radius, diameter, or circumference.

OUR APARTMENT ACTUALLY has a very nice kitchen. But the refrigerator has no solids in it, only condiments and drinks. And they're not even good condiments and drinks. We have two George Foreman grills (one with built-in bun warmer), a stove, a mini propane grill, a toaster, and a microwave. I don't think we've touched any of them even once. We cook so little that when we don't know where to put something and there is no room in the closet, we just stick it in the oven because it's never been used.

BRIAN IS AN investment banker, meaning he has one of the most warped outlooks of any twentysomething. It's amazing the kind of hours these people will work in exchange for a tote bag and a hat with the company logo on it that they'll never wear. And the expense account, that's where the real brainwashing comes in. Brian will come home from work and start bragging, "Karo, I expensed the sickest sushi dinner tonight!" I'll be like, "Wouldn't you have rather paid for your meal and not come home at 2 A.M.?"

IF I COULD use one word to describe the relationship between Brian and me, it would be "competitive." After all these years, we have not yet tired of trying to one-up each other. For instance, in our junior year of high school, I completely bombed a calculus test. Brian has kept my exam for eight years, and it now hangs on the refrigerator of our apartment. We once took an IQ test to determine who was smarter. When he beat me by a point, I declared the results null and void, seeing as his mom, who scored the test, was more biased than a French ice skating judge. And last year we made a hand-shake agreement that if either one of us ever won the lot-tery, we'd split it with the other. Mind you this was not to increase our chances of winning, but rather because neither of us could live knowing the other struck it rich first. I mean, I love the kid, but I ain't going out like that.

IT'S COMPLETELY AMAZING to me that Newton and Leibniz both invented calculus at the same time. I mean, fucking calculus. When Brian and I both had the same idea to have fajitas for dinner, we thought we might be psychic or something.

IN HIGH SCHOOL, my friend Eric bet Brian that he couldn't break 1400 on his SATs. Brian studied harder than he ever has in his life (whether this was to get into a good college or just win the bet, I'm still not sure). Regardless, he ended up getting exactly 1400. However, Eric claims that getting 1400 is technically not "breaking" 1400 and that a 1410 is needed to win the bet. This has become a point of contention for over nine years now, with no resolution in sight. In the spirit of reconciliation, and since I scored higher than both of them, I suggested that I should get the money. Somehow, that solved nothing.

BRIAN AND I have a stack of photos piling up on the IKEA coffee table in our apartment. Every photo has two things in common: both of us are in the picture and we only have one copy. Since we are unable to come up with a fair way to divvy them up, the pile just keeps growing. Brian's mom once asked him what we were going to do about the pictures when we move out. Brian replied, "Fight to the death?"

MOST TWENTYSOMETHINGS THINK that parents are amazing. As long as they're not your parents. When Brian's parents come to visit, he's a nervous wreck and invariably an argument ensues over dinner. Meanwhile, I'm totally relaxed, just enjoying the free meal and wondering why Brian is so uptight. Until my parents come. Then I'm a mess and can't wait for them to leave while stupid Brian is showing my mom my calculus test from eleventh grade.

THERE IS NO doubt in my mind that entering a relationship instantaneously changes your whole mentality. I'll never forget when that happened to Brian. On a Saturday morning at about 11 A.M., after an all-night rager, I stumbled out of bed to take a piss and was startled to find Brian sitting on the couch with the girl he had hooked up with the night before. And then it happened. He asked me if I wanted to get brunch with him and the girl. I was incredulous. "Brunch? Brunch?? Are you fucking kidding me? *Brunch?* What happened to the days when we used to get up at 2 P.M., get bacon, egg, and cheese sandwiches and 64-ounce lemon lime Gatorades, watch *SportsCenter,* and then go back to sleep for three more hours? *Brunch?* It's like I don't know you anymore. Don't you know that no single guys go to brunch? Anyway . . . could you, um, bring me back an omelet?" About a month later, Brian had a girlfriend and my life would change forever.

YOU HAVE TO understand my concern, though. Brian doesn't exactly have the best experience with serious relationships. A few months after we moved to Manhattan, he had such a falling out with his college girlfriend that they sent me as a neutral party to exchange belongings. He gave me all the clothes she had left at his place all nicely folded up. I met the ex-girlfriend at a prearranged location where she gave me all his stuff wrinkled up in a garbage bag. We then signed the obligatory treaty that, as Brian's best friend, I would never be able to hook up with her as long as I lived. It was all very official.

ANOTHER REASON I was concerned about Brian's new girlfriend is that it's my job. You see, in our group of friends, I am the highest-ranking single guy (meaning I have been single the longest). That means it is my duty to prevent my buddies who have girlfriends from becoming totally whipped. I feel like I am losing this battle. You know you're losing your friends to their girlfriends when they all start hanging out together as couples. Brian and his girlfriend had a dinner party a few weeks ago with a bunch of other couples. I overheard him on the phone talking to one of the guys and he actually said, "But my girlfriend likes red wine and yours likes white, what should we do?" I swear if he didn't pay half the rent I would have killed him right then and there.

I STARTED TO get really worried, though, when Brian brought his girlfriend to our friend's Super Bowl party. That is like the ultimate man-sin. I had to spend most of the first half fielding inane questions like, "Um, is the punt returner on offense or defense?" Darling, it's called special teams, now will you please get out of the way of the TV! To make matters worse, Brian bought his girlfriend boxes in our pool. Of course, she won the first three quarters. When a meaningless touchdown was scored with a few seconds left, preventing her from winning all the money, it was the most exciting moment of the entire day.

ALAS, AFTER A few months of Brian dating his girlfriend, I simply just gave up on him. It started harmlessly enough, with a Post-it note. When his girlfriend left the apartment one morning, she left him a little Post-it note that said something like "I love you. Have a great day!" OK, so that was pretty lame but I let it slide. Then I found another note the next day that read "I love you. Have a great day! XOXO." The next day the note didn't even have any words, it just said "XOXOXOXO." And just when I thought things couldn't get any worse, they did. I discovered it on a Wednesday, on his desk under a pile of love notes. A mix tape. They're making mix tapes for each other. Each one has a different "mood" when it's supposed to be played. Hmm, I wonder which one I should play when I'm feeling like my roommate is a pussy.

I HAVE TO say, though, that I'm happy for Brian and I've grown to like his girlfriend (and the brownies she makes me as a peace offering). It really looks like he's in a pretty solid relationship. At least most of the time. The kid is so neurotic about his girlfriend that when she came over unexpectedly one night, he literally dove across the room to hide a porno magazine in his gym bag. I'm like, dude, relax, I'm pretty sure she knows you beat off occasionally. Of course he forgot that his office searches everyone coming into the building. The next day a security guard pulled the magazine out of his bag in front of all of his co-workers.

BRIAN AND I regularly have a woman clean our apartment and do our laundry. I am not embarrassed by this—we are both financially independent and that's one perk we choose to spend our money on. What I am embarrassed about is that we decide to call the cleaning woman not when our apartment is sufficiently dirty, but when we run out of underwear. The problem is, we have different amounts of underwear and so an argument ensues every time. In order to ease tensions between us, we held an "underwear summit" where we both decided on a per day underwear allowance that would result in a mutually agreed upon laundry day. Cooler heads prevailed for a while until Brian's girlfriend broke the ceasefire by buying him a few new pairs, thus throwing off the balance of power. My ally, my mom, responded by buying me even more underwear, and now Brian and I are locked in a heated battle to stockpile the largest arsenal. It's like the Cold War of boxers.

THE OTHER NIGHT I realized just how much Brian and I are clueless bachelors. We had a couple of the guys over to have some drinks when someone spilled a beer on the carpet. As the Miller Lite flowed out of the bottle and onto our tattered rug, Brian and I stood paralyzed as we simultaneously came to the realization that we did not have one single paper product in the apartment. No paper towels, no toilet paper, no tissues, nothing. Without anything to absorb the spill there was nothing to do except blow vigorously until it soaked into the floor.

IF YOU THINK about it, apartment living in your early twenties is all about the strategic evolution of paper goods. Toilet paper becomes napkins. Napkins become paper towels. Paper towels become plates. And plates? Well, that's a luxury we just can't afford. The day after the Miller Lite debacle, Brian and I went to CVS to buy toilet paper. Since we were looking for maximum comfort at minimum cost, we stood there for fifteen minutes calculating and arguing over price per ply, double roll versus single roll, quilted, scented, etc. In the end, we just bought the package with the cutest baby on the front.

WHEN THAT TOILET paper ran out, another domestic crisis struck our apartment. Since Brian works many more hours than I do (or as Brian puts it, because he has a "real job"), it somehow became my implied responsibility to keep us stocked up on toilet paper. Fed up with this treatment, I didn't buy any more this time, but didn't say anything about it. I just left the last empty roll hanging on the dispenser and waited to see if Brian would go and buy more himself. But he never said anything. After a day or so, I got some rolls from our neighbors and hoarded them in my closet for my own use. A few more days of the TP embargo passed and Brian still hadn't said anything about it. Meanwhile, I had no idea what he was using in the bathroom. As Toilet Papergate reached Day Six, I considered sending a mutual friend as an emissary to talk to Brian's girlfriend about the situation. After a week, Brian finally asked me what the hell was going on. Apparently he had just been using tissues from his room. After much negotiation, consensus was reached, the embargo was lifted, and we agreed to split the responsibility in the future.

ONE THING ABOUT Brian really irks me. He inexplicably puts enormous bottles in our tiny bathroom garbage can. He'll finish an economy size shampoo that his mom bought him at Costco and jam it into our blue miniature IKEA garbage can, leaving no room for any other trash. And I can't convince him that what he's doing is wrong. It's like he's missing that part of his brain or something.

FOR BRIAN AND me, apartment maintenance is not exactly a top priority. Nowhere is this more evident than in the bathroom. Our bathroom has about half a dozen bulbs above the sink that light the room and make a half-hearted attempt at defogging the mirror. When the bulbs blow, they are not replaced. So, over the course of many months, our bathroom descends into total darkness. Only when we are reduced to shaving with candles do we get off our asses and head, reluctant and bloodied, to the hardware store. Whatever, light is overrated anyway.

ALSO IN OUR bathroom is a can of air freshener with the scent "Butterfly Garden." That's great, when someone takes a shit and uses the spray, it smells like someone took a shit in a butterfly garden.

BRIAN AND I use our cell phones so much that we don't even have a landline in our apartment. So now I have web-based email that I can check from anywhere and a cell phone. I'm completely virtual. Only thing is, when I come home after a long day, I have no emails or messages waiting for me. It's kind of anticlimactic.

THE FACT THAT I have a cell phone but no regular phone gets me in all sorts of trouble. Like the time I left my cell phone in my cousin's car. I didn't realize it until I had gotten back to my apartment. But Brian wasn't home so I literally had no phone to call anyone with. I was reduced to staring out my window, hoping I'd recognize someone in the street who I could holler to and ask to use their phone. After a fruitless hour of that, I finally formulated a plan. I opened the instant messenger on my computer. There was only one person on my buddy list online at the time, my friend in San Francisco. So I instant messaged him to call my parents who then emailed me to tell me that my neighbor was going to pick up the phone from my cousin and drive it into the city the next day where I could get it. Aren't cell phones convenient?

GUYS ARE REALLY proud of their dirty, disgusting baseball caps. I've been wearing the same beat-up New York Rangers hat for twelve years now. Once, the fire alarm went off in my apartment building and when we evacuated, I took my hat but forgot Brian was fast asleep in the other room. Funny thing was I think he was more angry that I didn't try to save his old Mets hat.

ONE THING I can always count on from my roommate is to keep me entertained with the funny shit that comes out of his mouth on a daily basis. Some of my favorites:

> Brian on his struggle to simultaneously stay in shape while working long hours to earn lots of money and then blow it all on clothes: "You know what would make me completely happy? If I could just weigh less than my jeans cost."

> Brian on one of the guiding principles of economics: "You know, Karo, a dollar today is actually worth less than a dollar tomorrow. Why? Because if I had a dollar today, I'd spend it!"

> Brian to our doorman after being told that the reason why he never recognizes us when we enter the building is that we're dressed differently today: "Dude, we dress differently every day."

Brian upset after breaking a jar of his favorite pickles all over the kitchen floor: "And the worst part is that I lost two pickles in the explosion. They were so young . . . barely even cucumbers."

Brian on being told by a cashier that the condoms he was buying were on sale for 50% off: "Half-price condoms? I don't like the sound of that. Why don't you just go ahead and charge me full price. Thanks."

WHILE BRIAN AND I might know a thing or two about condoms, feminine products are a whole other story. A while ago, Brian and I were talking to a few girl friends of ours and the topic came up. Apparently, and again, this is news to me, when women work together in an office for an extended period of time, eventually their, um, cycles synchronize so that they're all, you know, flowing at the same time. This both intrigued and frightened Brian and me, but we didn't think much of it. A few weeks later, we were sitting on the couch in our apartment, happily eating egg sandwiches and drinking Gatorade (his girlfriend was out of town), and we started to reminisce about some of the hijinks that have occurred in the years we've lived together. The story about long-term period synchronization came up and we both had a chuckle about the ridiculousness of the notion. A moment later, we simultaneously took the last bite of our respective sandwiches, licked our fingers, took a swig of Gatorade, leaned back on the couch, and sighed in perfect synch. Startled, we both looked at each other and Brian said, "Let's never speak of this again."

AND FINALLY, I recently realized how quick I am to pick a fight with my roommate. Because we both always eat out, the only thing resembling food that Brian and I ever keep in the apartment is a Brita pitcher. The other day I went into the refrigerator to pour myself a glass of water and I noticed that there was some turkey in a package on the shelf below the Brita. I was pretty pissed off. When Brian came home I was like, "I can't believe you're hiding food from me, I was starving the other day and I didn't think there was anything to eat!" Brian just stood there for a moment, looked at me quizzically, and then said, "So let me get this straight, Karo, are you actually accusing me of hiding food from you . . . in the refrigerator?" Fuck me.

TWO

the buddy system

Toward the end of my senior year of college, I started to feel like I needed a change. After all, for the past four years, I had been hanging out with the same fifteen people every day. We all went to the same bar, the same movie theater, and the same deli. I was ready to move on. So I moved to Manhattan where I now live within a ten-block radius of my entire crew from high school and about a dozen fraternity brothers. We all go to the same bar, the same movie theater, and the same deli. In other words, besides the 400% increase in my rent, not much has changed.

I soon learned that being surrounded by old friends isn't a bad thing. In fact, having a lot of friends around actually makes it easier to meet new people. And those new people sometimes know cute chicks. And that's a very good thing. Besides, by now the lines between my friends have become completely blurred. I've got high school friends, college friends, work friends, and friends I have no idea how the hell I met in the first place.

When a massive blackout struck New York City in the summer of 2003, the true nature of my friends was revealed. Many people pitched in to help during the crisis by directing traffic or assisting the elderly. But not my buddies. We headed directly to the only bar serving cold beer for blocks. But with ATMs not working, our funds quickly diminished, and a hearty few of us wandered through the darkened streets. Along the way, we stopped at apartments of friends throughout the city, who were quick to offer us their food, alcohol, and bathrooms. And as the lights flickered on many hours later, I realized that although you can't trust our nation's power grid, there's one network that's always there when you need it—the Buddy System.

THREE OF MY best friends are fraternal triplets. I've known them for most of my life and even went to Penn with two out of the three (hey, nobody's perfect, right?). I think one of the best parts about being a triplet is that you have built-in wingmen. All you have to do is go out with your brothers and you've already got two accomplices to help reel in the ladies. Since they don't look very similar, many times when I go out with all three of them people don't believe me when I tell them that they're triplets. I never understood this. What do you think I've got some sort of racket going where I go from bar to bar with three unrelated kids and pretend they're brothers?

THE TRIPLETS RECENTLY went on a cruise. They had a great time. Good for them. Except that they made friends on the boat that they've kept in touch with since. "Cruise friends" are the most annoying thing since "camp friends." The Triplets are always talking to them on the phone and meeting them out at the bar and exchanging pictures and making plans and shit. Dudes, please—what happens on the cruise, stays on the cruise!

EACH TRIPLET HAS a unique personality. Let me elaborate. Triplet #1 is a consultant who spends most of his free time watching the World Series of Poker on ESPN. He has an extensive collection of twenty-dollar Movados and Rolexes that he buys off the street. Triplet #1 also has the biggest cell phone I have ever seen, complete with a digital camera that takes pictures that never come out. He rarely cleans his plate, claims to have never had the hiccups, always forgets his glasses when we go to the movies, lives with Triplet #2, and is currently single. Triplet #2 is an investment banker with an enormous head. Literally. His skull is so large he needed to get a specially made helmet shipped in from Taiwan to play football in junior high. In high school, he fainted in Health class while watching *If These Walls Could Talk*. Triplet #2 is also a karaoke microphone-hogger, refusing to let anyone else participate as he belts Tracy Chapman songs from memory at the top of his lungs. He suffers from low-grade narcolepsy, always cleans his plate, and is also currently single. Triplet #3 is a med student who has a serious girlfriend. I go out with him the least of the three, but when we do go out he wears sneakers, thereby preventing us from getting in anywhere. Medicine is obviously in Triplet #3's blood. In high school, when an inebriated friend tripped and hurt his ankle, he rushed to the scene yelling, "Everyone out of the way, I know what I'm doing—my uncle is an orthopedic surgeon!" Triplet #3 has great hair, still lives at home, and is fond of stealing Triplet #1's fake watches. Some people ask me, "Karo, how do you remember who was born first?" That's easy, their initials are on their license plate in birth order. Triplet #2 isn't allowed to sit in the back, though. His head makes it difficult to see out the rearview mirror.

SOMETIMES BEING FRIENDS with triplets is really a pain in the ass because we can't go anywhere if they all come. If my roommate and I call them, it's five guys already and they won't let us in the club. Why couldn't they just be sisters?

SOME GUYS ARE just blessed with more game than others. I have one buddy in particular who possesses the one trait that all guys wish they had—the ability to get laid any night of the week. My friend Shermdog is impossible to track during the course of the night. You'll see blurry glimpses of him in the shadows hitting on chicks, but then he'll disappear without a trace, kind of like a khakis-clad Bigfoot. Then the next day he'll call and tell you some ridiculous story about the girl he took home. My friends are fond of saying that the two worst things you can hear in life are that your relative is in the hospital and that Shermdog knows your girlfriend from camp.

MY BUDDY CLAUDIO is one of my oldest and closest friends. He's also a bad-introducer. I'll be standing next to Claudio at the bar having a beer, and a succession of girls will come up, kiss him on the cheek, and make small talk, and he doesn't even acknowledge I exist. Unlike me, Claudio is friendly and nice, so he knows tons of people. But I've never met any of them.

THE WORST IS when I'm walking with Claudio and he bumps into someone in the street that he knows and starts to have a conversation with them but, as usual, doesn't introduce me. I have to do that little "awkward hover" where I stand one foot behind and to the right of them while they chat. And I feel like an idiot so I take my cell phone out of my pocket to check it even though it clearly didn't ring.

OF MY LAST two New Year's, one I spent in the hospital getting my appendix out and the other I spent in Vegas. This year, I'm looking for something right in between. From about June until the end of December, my friends and I will spend hours discussing, arguing, making, and revising our New Year's plans. But Claudio is by far the worst. Every year we make elaborate plans and then he cancels on us at the last minute because he has to celebrate his mom's birthday. We're like, dude, you've known the entire year that your mom was born on January 1st, why do you even make plans in the first place!?

SOMETIMES I WISH I had gone to a bigger school than Penn. Because I've pretty much met all the cute girls that I went to school with. Claudio went to Michigan, though, which is so big that he still meets hot chicks in New York that he graduated with but had never even heard of before. But does he introduce them to me? No.

GETTING OLDER CREATES the very weird experience of going to a bar in the city and ending up running into my friends' younger sisters. The situation is always the same. I'll be hanging out at a bar and I'll meet a cute girl who looks vaguely familiar. She seems to know me yet I can't figure it out. Then the kicker: "Oh, I'm Mike's sister, I met you when I visited the fraternity house four years ago." I immediately think, oh shit, then excuse myself, throw cold water on my face, and get the hell out of there!

I LOVE THE game of trying to guess who is calling you when an unfamiliar number comes up on caller ID. You'll be sitting around with your buddies and all of a sudden your cell phone rings and you're like, "Who is this? Area code 617? Where's that?" Then someone yells out, "Miami!" "Houston!" "San Diego?" "No, dog, that's Boston!" "Boston? Who do I know in Boston? Who could possibly be calling me from Boston? Should I pick it up?" "No, let it go to voice mail." "Boston, Boston . . . shit, it stopped ringing." "Who was it?" "They didn't leave a message." "I guess we'll never know."

THE REASON I won't pick up the phone is that I'm a notorious call-screener. When I first graduated, I couldn't wait to get a ring on my cell phone. Now I wield the "decline" button like it's nobody's business. Private number? You've got no shot. Even when I recognize the number, I send my friends straight to voice mail, just to show them who's boss. I was home at my parent's house over Thanksgiving and they don't have Caller ID. The phone rang and I almost broke into a cold sweat.

MY BUDDY ZACH is a long-message-leaver. When I check my voice mail and I hear it's him, I know I'm in it for the long haul. He's telling stories, he's making plans, he's telling me about this movie he saw, he's changing the plans, he's answering his landline, he's leaving his number even though I already have it. The guy leaves such comprehensive messages that there's almost no reason to call him back.

MY BUDDY ERIC is a shit-talker. These are the guys that are incapable of telling you a story without exaggerating. When you become close enough friends with a shit-talker, you learn to discount everything he claims by 75%. So if Eric claims he got a $20,000 raise and slept with four chicks last week, I know he only got a $5,000 raise and hooked up once. Tops.

MY BUDDY CHI is an unnecessary-drink-buyer. When 3 A.M. rolls around at the bar and you're nauseous and bloated, you can count on Chi to order two double rounds of the most disgusting shot available. Chi is also my male friend with the least knowledge of sports and holds the distinction of being the only person I know who used all his cell phone minutes for the month in one night by passing out drunk while on the phone. I guess he shouldn't have had that extra shot.

CHI IS ALSO a black belt. I think that's the coolest thing in the world. Whenever we go out and he gets really liquored up, I try to get him to kick someone's ass. Not just anyone, mind you, only people who deserve it, like bouncers or investment bankers. So far I've only gotten him to jump-kick a lamppost. The lamppost won.

SOMETIMES I WONDER who is lazier, Claudio or Chi. In Claudio's bathroom, he has one of those annoying toilet seats that won't stay up. He's so lazy, that instead of holding the seat up he actually sits down while taking a piss. Chi, on the other hand, once made the age-old mistake of opening a tab at the bar and then forgetting his credit card there. Instead of going back the next day, he just canceled it instead.

GUYS LIKE TO call their friends when they go to a sporting event just to brag about how they got free tickets. That's fine, but I hate when my buddies call me frantically to tell me to turn on the TV because they are behind home plate at the Yankees game or behind the bench at the Knicks game. I know you claim to be waving a giant foam hand right behind George Steinbrenner but I can't fucking see you. Please stop calling.

GUYS LIKE FREE tickets because buying them makes everything more complicated. Especially since my friends don't like to pay me back promptly. Last time I bought tickets, they made it as difficult as possible to recoup the money—they're trying to pay me all in quarters, writing nasty messages in the memo section of their checks, threatening not to pay until the moment the first pitch is thrown. It's really not fair. Then if you only have one other ticket, you're faced with the dilemma of who to take. For instance, if I score seats, my roommate usually automatically has first dibs. But last time I got tickets they were for a Yankees game. And he's a Mets fan. However, he did take me to an Islanders game last season. But I hate the Islanders. It's very complicated. You know what? From now on, I'm just going to take whoever pays me first!

I HATE THE Lakers, but I have to hand it to their fans. Because Lakers fans will watch every second of every game on TV. They could be up by thirty-seven points with sixteen seconds left in the game and my friend Ryan will be like, "Hold on, I just want to see if Kobe hits this free throw."

I THINK ONE of the most annoying questions you can ever be asked is "How was your trip?" You just got back from vacation and now you have to tell the same damn story over and over again to a bunch of people who don't really care. And every time you tell the story it gets shorter and shorter. My friend Kim traveled around the world for a full year. I felt really bad for her having to come up with an answer to that question for such a long trip. So when she got back, I asked her the only question I actually cared about: "Did you get laid?"

A LOT OF my buddies are really big gamblers. They're always playing poker or some card game for inordinate sums of money. I'm not a big gambler or a very good card player. But thankfully I have really good friends. They never make me feel left out. They're always encouraging me to play and offering to teach me how. They're even betting among themselves who can get me to play first. What nice guys.

IF YOU'RE ANYTHING like me, then you probably spend a good chunk of your day reply-to-all emailing with all of your buddies about what you did last night, what you're going to do tonight, and what you're doing this weekend. Some days, you're like the leader of the pack and you're replying to all the emails in like five seconds. And some days, when you're really busy, you get annoyed when yet another stupid email pops up. Have you ever not checked your email until like noon and when you do you have about fifty-seven messages, fifty of which are from your friends? You always feel like you missed something so you read every one before realizing that they were all just making fun of you for not emailing back.

FIVE OF MY closest friends are in medical school. Here's all you need to know about med school kids. They disappear for six to eight weeks at a time. During that time, the only human contact they have is with lab partners, Domino's deliverymen, and cadavers. When med school kids reappear, it is without notice. They just randomly show up at the bar one night, get drunker than everyone else, then pass out and disappear again. Med school kids also have no concept of money. However, I don't really blame them. If you're already close to a quarter of a million dollars in debt by the time you're twenty-four, I guess it's OK if your mom pays your cable bill.

I WISH MED school kids wouldn't show off so much. The other day a bunch of my friends were hanging out and someone farted. We all laughed but then Triplet #3 said, "Guys, that was just a natural mixture of carbon dioxide, formed from chemical reactions between stomach acid and intestinal fluid, as well as hydrogen and methane." Well, that kind of took the fun out of it.

I ALSO HAVE a lot of friends in law school. Here's what I know about law school kids. For some reason I feel immature around law school kids who are my age. I don't know why, maybe it's because the guys wear loafers and the girls have Palm Pilots. I do know this, though, law school kids bitch and moan more than any other grad students ("Oh my God, I have so much Contracts reading to do!"). Also, for some reason, I've noticed that once you enter law school, you're more likely to wear glasses (even though you've always had contacts), own a tie rack, and suddenly take up golf. So basically you become a loser.

WHAT IS IT about law school that attracts twentysomethings who have no interest whatsoever in studying law? I bet in the past month you've heard of at least one friend who has decided that they're going to law school. And your first reaction was probably, "Wait . . . what? Why?" Never in his life did your friend demonstrate any inkling of attending law school . . . until last week. Perhaps they don't understand that law school is not a hobby you just pick up one day. I think the law schools must have booths set up on the street that if you fill out an application you get a free towel or something. Or maybe your friend is just in it for the loafers and tie rack, I don't know.

TO ME, GRAD school is like camp. They take you on little trips, everyone still wears backpacks, you have all kinds of fun activities planned, and your day is over at like 4 P.M. On the totem pole of twentysomethings, I think grad school kids fall below the unemployed. Because at least the unemployed are resigned to their failure. Grad school kids are like the sore losers in the corner yelling, "Hey, no fair! Do over!"

A BUNCH OF people I know aren't in grad school, they just like taking entrance exams. First they took the GREs, then the GMATs, now they're on to the LSATs. They're like professional test-takers. These people also happen to live in the swankiest apartments, even though they don't have jobs. I wonder how they swing that.

DON'T YOU FIND yourself in conversation saying, "Wow, it's amazing what a small world it is!" more and more often these days? Just once I'd like to hear someone say, "Larry? Nope, never heard of him. Boy, this world is *huge!*"

I HATE IT when my friends make me wait for them so that we can leave together. We then proceed to walk down a flight of stairs together, go out the door, then go in completely opposite directions. What the hell was the point of that?

I WENT TO D.C. for July 4th weekend with a bunch of my frat buddies. Their thought process is hilarious. My friend Jen, who we were visiting, suggested we go to the White House. All of us at once were like, "Oh, is that a bar?"

MY BUDDY JEN is an e-card whore. She sends me an e-card for every single occasion—my birthday, Valentine's Day, President's Day, the autumnal equinox. It's wonderful because I know that she really cares. But I'm sort of frightened by the fact that she's able find so many different cards online that feature singing bears holding balloons.

JEN IS ALSO one of those people who has a perpetual pile of crap in the backseat of her car. It's always clothes she doesn't wear, books she hasn't read, and food she already ate. But it never goes anywhere, it just shifts positions. And the response is always the same: "Oh, just throw that stuff on the floor."

MY FRAT BUDDIES and I get together for a big steak dinner every once in a while. It's a fucking blast. We all tell ridiculous stories about chicks and then get called out for overexaggerating. The worst, though, is when the check comes. We always get into an argument over whether to itemize the bill or split it evenly. It's all game theory. If you think that the bill is going to be split evenly at the end, you go into the meal ordering extravagantly, but hope everyone doesn't do the same. If you think you're gonna itemize at the end, then you order conservatively but hope you don't have to contribute when your friend orders Grey Goose on the rocks with extra Grey Goose. Somehow, though, I always get stuck with a $100 tab when all I ate was a salad.

MY BUDDY DAVE, made famous in my first book for swinging Tarzan-style from a beer funnel across a forty-foot stairwell, recently continued his string of idiocy by going skydiving. Which I wouldn't have minded if he didn't make me watch the video. They always make you watch the video, don't they? And it's always the exact same thing. Dave getting harnessed up and looking all nervous. Dave still looking really nervous but giving the thumbs up sign as he is about to jump out. Dave flying through the air with his cheeks flapping giving the thumbs up sign again. For three minutes straight. To the *Top Gun* soundtrack.

SOME OF MY friends from college were what you might term "slackers." They did no work for four years. I don't know if it's just a coincidence, but they all happen to be from Los Angeles. I was having a drink with them in L.A. recently and I asked my friend if he wished he had studied harder at Penn. His answer was a vehement "no." He said, "Karo, what would doing more work have done for me? Maybe I would have learned more hard facts, but I wouldn't have learned more about applicating those facts, which is really more important." I replied, "Dude, applicating isn't even a fucking word."

I HAVE ANOTHER group of friends whose couch I stay on whenever I go out to Los Angeles. These guys all use either clay or paste products in their carefully styled hair. It's like a kindergarten classroom in their bathroom. They should probably be hanging out with those girls who put glitter on themselves. They could all get together, eat glue, and have a grand old time.

DO YOU HAVE friends who live with people that you're not friends with? When you call their apartment phone you hope the roommate doesn't pick up because then you are forced to have an awkward conversation about what you are doing that night even though they're not coming out with you and ask stupid questions about their day even though you don't really care and it's five minutes of your life that you will never get back and next time you think you'll just call your friend's cell phone instead.

MY BUDDY GADI went to culinary school. Now there is a noble vocation. The only time I use a kitchen utensil is to stir a mixed drink, so I am completely in awe of what he learned. And he doesn't disappear for months on end like med schools kids, bitch and moan like law school kids, or mooch off his parents like professional test-takers. There are no cadavers, standardized entrance exams, loafers, or tie racks, just funny chef hats and damn good food. Now that, my friends, is living.

BEFORE CULINARY SCHOOL, Gadi served in the Israeli Army. We went out for a few drinks the other night. He gave me some really great perspective on things. When we left the bar, I thought, you know, this guy really has his head on his shoulders. Then we realized his car was gone. The spot where he parked was actually marked "NYPD Parking Only" and he got towed. And this is a guy who used to drive a tank.

AFTER CULINARY SCHOOL, Gadi became a trance music DJ (yes, I know, he's more interesting than the rest of my friends combined). As you can imagine, trance is not really my scene, but I went to one of his shows to support him. It was actually pretty cool. The place was bumping, the music was much better than I expected, and the crowd was into it. I will tell you this much, though, I was definitely the only person there wearing Banana Republic socks.

SOME OF MY buddies are obsessed with fantasy sports to the point that I'm actually worried about them. My friend Jeremy told me he was at this club and bumped into Kurt Thomas, a forward on the Knicks. Now if I met Kurt Thomas, I'd be getting his autograph, taking pictures with him, etc., but not Jeremy. Here is their conversation. Jeremy: "Hey, you're Kurt Thomas!" Thomas: "Yeah." Jeremy: "It's great to meet you." Thomas: "Thanks, dog." Jeremy: "You know, I have you on my fantasy basketball team." Thomas: "Word?" Jeremy: "Yeah. Listen, I was wondering if I could ask you a favor." Thomas: "What?" Jeremy: "I'm in second place and I could really use some more blocks from you." Thomas: "More blocks? No doubt, I'll see what I can do." Jeremy: "Thanks man, have a good night." A few days later, Thomas set a career-high for blocks in a game.

I GUESS I understand why Jeremy has so much time to focus on fantasy sports. He partied so hard in college that he actually did permanent damage to his liver and now has to keep his alcohol intake to a minimum. Of course, every time I go out with him I totally forget about his condition halfway through the night. I'm always like, "What's up dude!? What's going on!? Oh shit, wait, I forgot, wait, you're sober, right? Wow, that's uh, that's, that really sucks. You want an ice water or something?" Yeah, he doesn't call me too much anymore.

MY BUDDY NICK is thirty, which to me, is incredibly old and wise. Whenever I ask him about women, he pushes the relationship side of the argument. He believes that the stability and security of a girlfriend far outweigh the debauchery of the single life. Then I found out that he's been engaged twice but never married. That's just great, I'm getting dating advice from a guy who's got more rings than Warren Sapp.

MY BUDDY ROB is always trying to set me up. At first I thought he was one of those guys whose judgment you could definitely trust. He really hyped up the first date he set me up on. It was a bust. The second chick he suggested was even worse. I've now been forced to downgrade him to "secondary confirmation status." I need at least one other trustworthy guy to see the girl before I spend a dime on her.

MY BUDDY JON brings his own drink when we go out to lunch. He says what restaurants charge for drinks is outrageous and they don't always have the soft drinks he prefers. Seriously, we'll all sit down and order beverages and he'll calmly put his own can of soda on the table. And the only thing I'm thinking is that we better not be itemizing this meal, because this is some bullshit.

MY BUDDY SETH was dating this girl for about a year when one day they got into a huge fight over the phone and both hung up in a huff. They never spoke again. That's it, no discussion, no reconciliation, no official break-up, nothing. I was like, "Dude, you can't do that, you have to talk to her, you went out for a year!" Seth said, "Why? Forget it, we're through." I pleaded, "Seth, do it for me, please. She had hot friends. Damn it, *I* need closure!"

MY BUDDY ADAM has a little different approach. When he was caught red-handed kissing another blonde at a dark club, he actually told his girlfriend, "But I thought it was you!"

IN THE END, the one drawback of the Buddy System is the constant amount of peer pressure being placed upon you. For instance, since graduation I've partied like a wild animal in Manhattan, South Beach, Hollywood, Las Vegas, Mardi Gras, Glasgow, and Rio de Janeiro. I've spent thousands of dollars on alcohol and admission to alcohol-dispensing facilities. I've hooked up a lot and been shot down even more. I've thrown up on myself and others. But when one of my buddies calls me at midnight on a rainy Tuesday to see if I want to grab a beer and I decline, the response is always the same: "Karo, you're a pussy." Fuck me.

THREE

seeing single

To me, single women in their twenties are like a preseason football game—it may seem like they're trying to score, but really they just don't want to get hurt. On the other hand, single men are like the Super Bowl—they're always trying to go all the way like it's the last chance they'll ever get. This seemingly small difference in thinking leads to an extraordinary amount of waste being generated by single men and women who have absolutely no clue what the other wants. Money is wasted, time is wasted, and next thing you know it's 4 A.M. on Saturday night and you're alone . . . and wasted.

The way I see it, girls go out looking for guys the same way they shop. They like to look at all the options at length. They browse. They compare. And when it's all said and done, they're just as happy to go home empty-handed. For guys, it's really tough to convince a girl to buy what you're offering. Women are like Hollywood executives and NBA point guards—they're looking for any reason to pass.

When my very first girlfriend broke up with me, I was quite upset. I told my dad I just didn't understand women. My dad responded, "You don't understand women? I don't understand women. Women don't even understand women! Just give up." And you'd think I had—I did the math and calculated that I spent roughly 82% of my early twenties single, including four consecutive years. But it was probably the best 82% of my entire life.

Go to any bar and you're bound to see the mating ritual happening in pairs—two guys who've had two too many drinks circling the outskirts of the dance floor with two dollars combined left in their wallets staring at the two girls at the bar clutching two overpriced handbags and ordering two more apple martinis. But don't worry, you're not seeing double, you're seeing single.

TWENTYSOMETHING GUYS HAVE a few steadfast rules when it comes to the opposite sex. Our first rule is never go out on a date on a weekend night if you're not sure you're going to hook up. If things go sour, you've wasted 50% of primetime for nothing. Second, always go out for drinks on the first date. Dinner's way too expensive, especially if the only piece you're gonna get is a sirloin. Third, try to delay hanging out sober for as long as possible. While relatively inexpensive, the first sober hang-out is usually awkward and could possibly lead to hooking up sober, which can get tricky if you haven't done it in a while. Finally, and probably most importantly, once you hook up with a girl, whatever you did in bed is reasonably expected to be the minimum of what you do the next time. Hey, I don't make the rules, I just follow them!

WHEN YOU ASK a girl out, the way she rejects you can be very telling of how she really feels. Like if you leave a message and she emails you instead of calling back, that's bad. But the most important thing to look for is the "alternate day suggestion." For instance, I asked a girl out for a Thursday night once and she said, "Actually, I already have plans, but thanks for asking." See, there was no alternate day suggestion. Which basically means "drop dead." On the other hand, if she would have said, "Actually, I already have plans, but how about Friday?" that implies she's interested. Of course, I'd have to decline the offer since Friday is a weekend and that's against the rules.

ALSO BE WARY of any email from a girl that begins with the word "listen." Chances are, it's going to be bad and involve the words "really" and "but." "Listen, I had a really great time, but I'm getting back together with my boyfriend." "Listen, you seem really sweet, but I don't think this is going to work out." I now automatically delete any emails that start with "listen" because I kept getting my hopes up with "really" and crushed with "but."

A LOT OF my friends say they like a "challenge." You know these guys. They're like, "I don't care if she's engaged, it's more fun that way, I like the challenge." Me, I don't want to be challenged. I don't have the energy for that. I'm looking for a single girl. I don't want challenges, obstacles, or hurdles, thank you very much.

I WAS TALKING to a girl in a bar recently and she told me she was excited because she had a date the next night with a guy who had "The List." "The List?" I asked. "Yeah," she said, "he's got everything a girl wants in a guy," and went on to name them—attractive, smart, funny, right religion, good job, nice family, etc. As we continued the conversation, I realized that she was talking about a blind date and that her friend was setting her up. I was like, "Are you kidding me? Every guy has The List *before* you meet him! Hell, I've got six friends with The List on the way right now!"

SOME OF MY single friends have started to diversify themselves a little bit. My buddy Claudio was hooking up with a thirty-five-year-old marketing executive. I asked him how the sex was. He was like, "Who cares, she's a vice president!"

DATING OLDER CHICKS is always made more fun by retroactively applying the age gap. You're like, well, when she was a senior in college, I was, let's see, a freshman in high school. Holy crap . . . I'm the man!

RECENTLY, I'VE BEEN running into a perplexing breed—girls still dating their boyfriends from college. You know how this generally works: they've been dating on-again off-again since sophomore year, he cheated on her, she took him back, they took some time off after graduation but now they're back together because she can't be alone, it'll never work out long-term but it's convenient for now, blah, blah, blah. Ladies, guys, it's time to move on, free up some ass for the rest of us.

HERE'S SOMETHING I'VE been pondering. When it rains on a weekend night, where the fuck is everybody? The bars are like ghost towns. Now I know all the couples are snuggling up at home watching Hugh Grant movies, but where are the single people? This is our time to shine! Throw on those North Faces and get out here!

AND ONCE YOU hit the bar, you immediately attempt to meet a girl and convince her to leave with you against her better judgment. The worst is when you get in a cab with a girl at the end of the night and right away she tells the cabbie, "Two stops"—meaning one for her and one for you and your right hand. I once went home with a girl who told the cabbie to go to my block. I was psyched until she bolted from the cab and into her apartment—which just happened to be across the street.

SINGLE GUYS HAVE an intricate system for scouring a bar for prospects. We usually use a two-man formation. One guy is the designated "wingman" whose primary responsibility is to find and initiate conversations with hot chicks. Once the wingman has established a position, he transitions his friend into the conversation and then reports back to the other guys. When describing the attractiveness of a girl to his friends, guys will sometimes use the "beer rule," which is the number of beers one would have to drink in order to hook up with a girl. Anyone less than a six-pack is pretty good. Anyone over a twelve-pack will just make for a funny story the next day.

ONE THING THAT twentysomethings have in common with college kids is that we spend a lot of our time randomly hooking up, rather than actually dating, which inevitably leads to the dreaded process of having to break up with someone without ever having gone out with them in the first place. Generally, guys accomplish this task via the "phase-out." I had been hooking up with this girl for about a month when I suddenly realized that both Valentine's Day and her birthday were only six weeks away. And once gift acquisition takes place, you're automatically on the hook for at least another month, so I quickly implemented a phase-out. First, I began transferring communication from phone to email. Then, I cut our weekend hang-out frequency by 50%. She probably never even realized it was happening. Finally, with only two weeks to go before V-Day, I deleted her out of my cell phone and stopped emailing. Phase-out complete!

SO MY COUSIN was dating this girl for a while. He was pretty into her, but then she left him for another guy. Eventually, the girl ended up marrying this new guy. My cousin was pretty bummed. I think the fact that she ended up marrying this guy should have cheered him up. It's kind of like if the Knicks lose in the playoffs, but the team that beat them goes on to win the championship. At least you lost to the best, you know?

I ALWAYS FIND it amusing when I'm talking to a chick in a bar and it turns out that she's there with a guy she's hooking up with. And the guy wants to make it very obvious that he's with the girl so he marks his territory—he's putting his arm around her, he's holding her hand, all while I'm still trying to have a conversation. I'm like, take it easy, dude, why don't you just lift your leg and piss on her shoes while you're at it?

FOR SOME REASON, women I meet are always asking me to guess how old I think they are. But the worst possible thing I can do is guess too high and offend them. I met this girl at a bar once and she asked me to guess how old she was. I was like, "Uh, eight?"

THE OTHER DAY, I ran into one of my least favorite types of girls: the boyfriend-mentioner. The boyfriend-mentioner finds a way to bring up her boyfriend in just about every sentence she utters, even if you're not hitting on her. "My boyfriend thinks this, my boyfriend did this, my boyfriend said this." And I'm thinking, no wonder your boyfriend isn't here, you're really fucking annoying!

HOW TO LOSE a Guy in Ten Seconds at the Bar: tell me how much you enjoy being an investment banker, take a drag off your lipstick-stained Parliament, ask me if your fake ID looks real, mention your boyfriend who just got drafted by the Bears, discuss your opposition to premarital sex, order a mixed drink with Diet Coke, explain why you like both the Mets and Yankees equally, or tell me how you really have to get home tonight . . . to New Jersey.

GUYS LOSE CLOTHES when they get ass. Whenever a girl leaves my place in the morning and asks for something to wear, I always give her my most expendable shirt because I know I'm never getting it back. It's like a sacrifice to the hook-up gods.

GUYS AREN'T BIG on long-distance relationships. A friend asked me why I didn't get serious with this girl I was hooking up with in Philadelphia. I was like, are you kidding me? I won't even date a chick on the Upper West Side.

GUYS DON'T CARE if a girl's place is messy. Ever go home with a girl and she makes you stand outside her door while she "tidies up?" Listen, we're just happy to be there. And if there are bras and panties everywhere, even better!

THE FEW TIMES I've showered at a girl's apartment have confused the hell out of me. Have you noticed that the gels, lotions, and shampoos found in women's bathrooms always come in some sort of scent that doesn't actually exist in nature? It's like vanilla grapefruit, green tea blackberry, and mango teriyaki. Also, did I miss the poof revolution? Since when did it become mandatory for all girls to use a purple poofy thing to lather up in the shower? Guys were just not meant to use a poof. It's too rough in places it should be gentle and too gentle where it should be rough. I feel uncomfortable just writing about it.

ANOTHER STRAIN OF female I have learned to be wary of is the girl who has no girl friends. Advantages: tends to party harder than your standard chick, more likely to let you spend time doing guy things (i.e., playing video games and watching *SportsCenter*). Disadvantages: doesn't bring out other hot chicks for your friends, more likely to be surrounded by dudes at all times. Conclusion: If she's less than a six-pack, definitely a keeper.

HAVE YOU EVER hooked up with someone who actually worked in a bar? I used to hook up with this bartender chick. I never knew what to tip her. Too little and I wouldn't get laid, too much and she felt like a prostitute. It was so much stress that I eventually had to perform a phase-out and just hope my friends never wanted to go to that bar again.

ONCE I WENT out and got drunker than a guest on *Jimmy Kimmel Live.* I met a cute brunette and at the end of the night we went back to my apartment. As things were getting hot and heavy, she casually remarked that she thought my bedroom looked familiar. A few minutes later, I said I thought that *she* looked familiar. Then we both realized it. We had actually gone home together a year earlier but both of us were too drunk to remember it. That's right, folks, I'm hooking up in reruns.

HOW COME WOMEN consistently list the number-one trait they are looking for in a guy as "sense of humor," but when I say I'm a comedian they look at me like I'm a janitor?

IS IT WEIRD that when I am introduced to two people who are going out the first thing I do is imagine them fucking?

SEVERAL OF MY friends have serious girlfriends. I am single. I think my friends who have girlfriends have forgotten what it is like to be single. Their whole incentive system is off. We'll be at a bar and they'll want to stay and I'll want to leave. They'll be like, "Yeah, this is a great bar, I've got my girl and I've got my buddies, what more can you ask for?" I'll be like, "Dude, I'm glad you're having such a great time but your girlfriend is the only chick in here and I'm trying to get laid. See ya."

I LOVE HOW every ridiculous model featured in a racy spread in *Maxim* magazine always has that quote next to her picture that says something like, "I was a total flat-chested dork in high school and no guys would talk to me." Where the fuck is this high school?

THERE'S JUST SOMETHING about smelling your ex-girlfriend's perfume. When I meet a girl and she's wearing the perfume my ex-girlfriend used to wear, it always involuntarily brings back a flood of memories—the laughter, the joy, the screaming matches, the name-calling. Of course, I still have no idea what exactly the name of the perfume she wears is. Wait a minute, is that something I was supposed to know?

I THINK THAT the phrase "It's girls' night out" is the new version of "I'm washing my hair" when it comes to lame excuses why a girl can't go out with you. Women act like "girls' night out" is some sort of secret, sacred ritual. But

I think I know what's going on. It's a dozen girls in uncomfortable heels going to an overpriced restaurant where everyone orders a salad or the tuna, the last three guys that each girl hooked up with is given an official nickname, at least one dish gets sent back, everyone gets tipsy off of two glasses of white wine, the bill is paid on twelve different American Express cards and then everyone leaves and calls each other on their cell phones to gossip about all the other girls. See, I know what's up.

ANOTHER HALLOWEEN, THE second easiest night of the year to hook up, has passed and yet again I did the walk of shame in the wee hours of November 1st looking ridiculous. In *Ruminations on College Life*, I set forth my first rule of Halloween—that no matter what her costume is supposed to be, every girl basically dresses like a whore. Now I'd like to add a second rule. No matter what you're wearing on Halloween, there will always be one part of your costume that bothers the hell out of you all night. For me, it was the stupid belt on my army man outfit that kept coming apart. Given the amount of time I spent at the bar trying to fix my belt instead of hitting on women dressed like whores, it's astonishing I was able to do the walk of shame at all.

A FEW MONTH'S later on New Year's Eve, the easiest night of the year to hook up, I managed to make it back to a girl's place even though I was completely plastered. Just when things were getting hot and heavy, I blurted out, "So is your roommate around?" She was like, "Asshole, I live in a studio."

VALENTINE'S DAY IS depressing for some. Couples are out in force. Love is in the air. They even turn the lights atop the Empire State Building red for the day. But being single for so long has taught me a valuable lesson: Valentine's Day is a great day to get ass, third only to New Year's Eve and Halloween. Think about it: all the girls at the bar are single and they're probably lonely. Just commiserate a little about how depressing the day is, maybe mention the Empire State Building, buy her a couple of cocktails, and you're in. So stop moping and take advantage!

IS IT POSSIBLE to lie in bed with a girl after hooking up and not have at least one of your arms fall in some awkward and uncomfortable yoga-style position where the girl says, "Is your arm OK?" and the guy lies and says, "Yeah, it's fine"?

WHY IS IT that you can be naked hooking up with a chick all night but when she gets up in the morning to put her bra on she turns her back to you?

I WAS AT this bar once talking to a cute girl. I made a joke and she laughed really hard. I thought to myself, good work, Karo, nice joke. Then the girl said, "Oh, I laugh at everything." That's great, way to shatter me.

YOU GOTTA LOVE the preemptive cheek kiss. You know, like at the end of the night at the bar or at the end of a date at the girl's door? She wants to make clear she has no intention of hooking up so she squeaks "Good night!" and jams her cheek in your face so you have no chance whatsoever of making lip contact. It's a move guys have yet to come up with a defense for.

SOMETIMES WE SINGLE twentysomethings have to beware of imposters. I was at a bar having a conversation with this girl who was a few years older than me, but she still seemed interested. Then she scratched her face. A glare caught me right in the eye. And then I saw it. A diamond ring. Frightened, I said, "What the hell is that?" "Oh, this? I just got engaged last week."

"Engaged? What the hell are you doing here then?"
"Well, my fiancé is meeting me here later." And that's when I realized that from now on, I have to Look for the Ring. This sucks. All I know is, someone should tell the guy at the door not to let married people in.

I WAS REALLY into this girl but there was nothing I could do about it because she's a textbook Serial Monogamist. You know these girls, right? They somehow go from boyfriend to boyfriend without ever really dating in between. I don't know how that's physically possible. I'm gonna wait for an opening, though, and get back to you on this one.

I THINK THE way you can tell if a guy and girl are in a serious relationship is whether or not they have black-and-white pictures of themselves frolicking in a field or at the beach or some bullshit like that. That's the real test. Because it takes effort to get nice black-and-white pictures, we ain't talking mall photo booth shots anymore. Once you're in a field taking pictures, there's no turning back.

I HATE PEOPLE who track the length of their relationship way too precisely. "So how long have you and Sara been dating?" "Oh, about twenty months." What is she, a fucking newborn?

I LOVE LISTENING to my girl friends talk about the new guy they are hooking up with. They'll be like, "Oh my God, this boy is so cute. We talk on the phone for like four hours every night!" What? Who has time to talk on the phone that long? And who has that much to say? Guys, whichever one of you out there is doing this, please stop. You're ruining everything.

HAVE YOU EVER been out with your parents and you happen to run into the girl you've been randomly hooking up with and you're forced to introduce everyone? As soon as the girl leaves you can tell your mom is all excited and she's like, "Well, she seemed nice—" and you have to quickly cut her off and then carefully explain the difference between "hooking up" and "going steady" and finally break the news that, most likely, that's the last time she's ever going to see that girl again.

LIKE CLOCKWORK, EVERY Saturday night at about 4 A.M. on the streets of Manhattan you will see dozens of single guys walking solemnly down the sidewalk, their spirits broken, their shirts ruffled, and their wallets empty. They have left the bar without hooking up and are now trudging back to their tiny apartments alone. I call these unfortunate men the "Lost Souls." I have been a Lost Soul many a night. I usually use this time to ponder life's great mysteries. Like what exactly is cilantro? Why do different shapes of pasta taste differently? What is the purpose of DVD reviews, isn't it going to be the same as the movie itself? Does anyone ever actually use the vosotros form in Spanish? Do motorcycles have radios? Where do valets actually park your car? If you can't feed Gremlins after midnight, then when can you feed them? Why do weathermen and dentists always have funny nicknames like Dr. G? What is Ralph Macchio doing at this very instant? Why are there more personnel at the airport helping people who can't figure out how to use the "self-service" e-ticket machines than anywhere else? Are there any accidents not caused by overturned tractor-trailers? Did I leave the Foreman grill plugged in? You know what, I think I need a girlfriend . . .

I GUESS I shouldn't be too surprised that single men and women have such a hard time getting together.

We're just so different. Girls dream about meeting that one great love. Guys fantasize about the Olsen twins and the Hilton sisters . . . at the same time. Girls have all the pictures they have ever taken in their lives organized by genre on Ofoto. Guys say they'll make doubles of that picture of you puking on yourself but never actually do. Girls spend their free time shopping for shoes, hair products, and nonfat frozen yogurt. Guys spend their free time deciding who to play at wide receiver on their fantasy football team when the Giants have a bye week. Girls spend all of their hard-earned money on clothes that aren't warm enough, shoes that hurt their feet, and online horoscopes that they follow way too closely. Guys spend of all their hard-earned money trying to have sex with girls. But despite all the pitfalls of being single, when I go to the bar with my single buddies and look around at all the beautiful single women around me, I can't help but smile, take out a single, tip the bartender, and say, "Hey, make that a double."

SOMETIMES, THOUGH, WHEN you've been seeing single too long, you forget to pay attention to detail. I met this girl Jamie and I wanted to take her out one night so I gave her a call during the day. We made plans to go out later and I was supposed to call her at 8 P.M. Eight o'clock rolls around and I call, but her voicemail picks up. I tell her to give me a call back. She doesn't. Eight-fifteen rolls around, I give her another call, there's no answer, so I hang up. Eight forty-five comes and I'm fuming, thinking I've been stood up. I give her a call again, her voicemail picks up again, and I leave a somewhat pissed off message. I never fucking hear from the girl. She stood me up. She never calls. Not the next day or the day after that. About a week later I get a call from a friend of mine who lives in Tennessee. I'm chatting with her and then she says, "Oh yeah, last week you left these two strange messages on my phone about getting together, what the heck were you talking about?" Then I realize it. Her name is Jamie too. I have two Jamies in my cell phone. Every time I called that night I called the wrong Jamie. I never actually called the girl I wanted to take out. She thinks I stood *her* up! Fuck me.

FOUR

nocturnal admission

New York is home to countless bars, clubs, as well as lounges. "Lounge" is actually a term originally coined to refer to an establishment combining the most annoying attributes of both bars and clubs but sporting a catchy monosyllabic name. Whatever your preferred venue, though, partying in your early twenties is a unique and incredible experience. If you know where to go. And you can get in. And you can afford it. And you avoid the puddles of vomit in the street.

Every holiday season, I receive tons of emails from fans around the world who are visiting the Big Apple for the first time. It seems as if I am considered a connoisseur of nightlife in the city because I frequently write about my alcohol-induced exploits. The one question I get most often from out-of-towners is this: "Karo, where's a good place to go out?" And after a few minutes of stammering and racking my brain, I usually respond, "You know what, man, I have no fucking clue." The thing is, there are millions of interesting people who party in the city. Unfortunately, most of them are waiting on line in front of you.

When the sun sets on Friday night, one species emerges as the dominant breed—single twentysomethings bent on inebriation and fornication. While these objectives are nothing novel to us (after all, we've been partying and mating for the better part of a decade at this point), the way we go about achieving these objectives has changed. Each weekend night in the inexorable march toward our late twenties is marked by higher stakes—the alcohol more costly, the women more choosey, and the nagging suspicion in the back of our minds that there's more to life than binge-drinking and laying pipe. I'm not ashamed to admit that, for me, the weekend remains an opportunity for release, both mentally and, well, you get my gist. This is my nocturnal admission.

THE FIRST DECISION that single men must make is what bar to go to in order to pick up women. This decision is usually made over many drinks while pre-gaming with the boys at someone's apartment. Inevitably, you decide on a place where one of your buddies "heard there were gonna be a ton of hot chicks." That this has never once been true does not deter us. The fact is, drunk, single guys go to annoying bars for the same reasons weary travelers fly into Newark Airport—it's out of the way, it's inconvenient, but you weren't thinking straight and it seemed like a good idea at the time.

YOU CAN'T SURVIVE in Manhattan without a cell phone, at least on the weekends. It's all a game of meeting up, getting together, going out, and getting smashed. Since the bars don't close until the wee hours of the morning, the next day I tend to find myself hungover and confused. I've found that by examining the outgoing and incoming call logs on my cell phone, I'm able to piece together where I was and who I was with between the hours of 10 P.M. and 5 A.M. It's kind of like *CSI: New York.*

NO TWENTYSOMETHING IN the nightlife scene is more skilled in the art of hyperbole than the promoter. Promoters are paid by clubs and lounges to attract people to their establishments, usually via an unsolicited barrage of calls, emails, text messages, and crazily ornate flyers featuring Japanimation cartoons of scantily clad women who, if they really existed, wouldn't go within a hundred yards of said establishment. Never ask a promoter if a party is actually going to be good because this is the answer you're bound to receive: "It's going to be off the heezie. Seriously, dude, off the heezie. There's not even going to be any more heezie after this party, man." Um, OK, I think I'm just going to stay home and jerk off to this flyer instead.

THE FACT THAT bars, clubs, and lounges have become the arena for single mating puts guys at a serious disadvantage. For one thing, we can't get in unless we're with girls. But if we were with girls, we wouldn't be going in the first place. This leads to the desperate measure of getting on your cell phone and calling girls that you know are inside to come out and convince the bouncer to let you in. And when that embarrassing situation is finally over, you get inside and usually head straight for the bathroom—where you are forced to piss in a trough filled with ice. So I've been out of the house for about twenty minutes, I haven't even hit on anyone yet, and

I've already been completely emasculated. I should have just left my balls at home.

A WHILE AGO I went to this lounge but was quickly barred from entry by the bouncer who kindly told me that there was too much "sausage" inside. As I stood helplessly on line, I happened to see my ex-girlfriend Dina walking by. I convinced her to get on line with me and pretend she was still my girlfriend so I could get in. Then we started fighting on the line. I said she was too clingy, she said I don't listen to her (at least that's what I think she said). By the time we got inside the bar, we had broken up all over again. The important thing, though, is that I got in.

NEVER MEET YOUR friends out at the bar unless you know exactly where the bar is. Because once your friends get hammered, the odds of them being able to direct you to a dive with no sign off an alley on First Avenue are slim to none. Drunk friends can't even comprehend why you can't find the bar. They're like, "Karo, what do you mean you can't find the bar? We're *in* the bar . . . we're in the bar right now, just come inside!"

IN ORDER TO party most effectively in your early twenties, you need to know four very important things: the Art of the Nap, the Art of the Pre-Game, the Art of the Drunk Dial, and the Art of Late-Night Eating.

THE ART OF the Nap. Naptime in New York is generally from 8 to 9 P.M. When you wake up, you are required to say things like, "Oh, I feel horrible" or "Man, I could easily go right back to sleep for the whole night." Fight through it. You'll need that nap to get all the way to late-night eating.

THE ART OF the Pre-Game. The pre-game (also know as pre-drink or pre-bar) is a money-saving skill I learned in my fraternity days. When you're pre-gaming at a buddy's apartment, there's always that roommate who doesn't feel well or has to go to work the next day and is trying to get some sleep so he emerges groggily from his room to ask everyone to be quiet and you comply but within a few minutes, the noise level involuntarily returns to its previous intensity, causing the roommate to ask for quiet yet again and the futile cat-and-mouse game continues until the roommate finally just gives up and waits for you assholes to leave and go to the damn bar already.

THE ART OF the Drunk Dial. The proliferation of cell phones in recent years has made the drunk dial an almost unavoidable occurrence. The doorway of the bar, where it's not too loud, freezing, or sweltering, is the perfect breeding ground for the three varieties of drunk dial. First, you have your Bragging Call, which consists of calling everyone in your phone book to tell them how drunk you are even though no one you call can hear a word you're slurring. Then you have the Booty Call, which usually goes something like this: "Hey, girl, long time no speak, it's about um, let's see . . . three forty-five A.M. Wanna hang out?" Then you have the Boner Call, which is the dumb-ass message you leave on your ex-girlfriend's or parent's machine. You usually hear about those the next day.

THE ART OF Late-Night Eating. Late-night eating happens like this: you get up from your nap like, "Shit, I'm kinda hungry right now." You start pre-gaming and promise, "Dude, I'm not eating late-night again tonight." You get to the bar like, "Well, if I hook up tonight, I won't be able to eat." Next thing you know you're leaving a message on your ex-girlfriend's voice-mail and saying to the cashier, "I'll have two pepperonis and a white slice to go, please."

IF YOU'RE GONNA go out in New York, you have to talk the talk. Terms you need to know: Cover, Promoter, Comped, Guest List, VIP, and Reduced Admission. "Cover" is the charge you pay at the door just to get in the club. In business school terms, the purpose of the cover is to increase customer switching costs, i.e., once you pay twenty bucks to get in somewhere that sucks, you're less likely to leave and go somewhere else. "Promoter," which I previously described and is also known as the "Clipboard Guy," is hired by the club to tell everyone they know about a party and then stand outside and not let anyone in. "Comped" means the promoter told you that you would get in for free, but when you get there you're not on the "Guest List" he has on his clipboard and you have to pay anyway. "VIP" and "Reduced" mean the same thing—absolutely nothing!

EVER SPY A girl opening her purse to get money at the bar? Twenties and ones are flying everywhere, there's no rhyme or reason. It's a good thing that girls can get guys to buy them drinks because I'm not sure that a crumpled mass of bills sandwiched between two vats of lip gloss is considered acceptable currency.

I'M SICK OF hearing about "my friend's band." It seems like every weekend someone is saying to me, "Hey, I'm going to see my friend's band, you should come, they're really good!" And they're always playing in some out-of-the-way shithole and the only people that like them are . . . their friends. You know, come to think of it, "My Friend's Band" is actually a pretty cool name for a band. I just hope I never get invited to see them play.

I LOVE WHEN guys ask the bartender what draft beers are available and then think really profoundly about which one to select like they a) can really tell the difference and b) don't realize that every tap is usually connected to a Coors Light keg anyway.

WHY DO ALCOHOLIC beverages list the awards they won like four hundred years ago? It seems like every imported beer or vodka I drink won some sort of medal in the 1600s. Is that really still a selling point?

THE FACT THAT, unlike most cities, bars in New York are open until at least 4 A.M. helps mitigate the occurrence of what I call "last call surprise." Last call surprise occurs at the end of the night when the bartender announces last call and flicks the light on, thereby revealing the girl you've been hitting on for the past hour in all her horrible glory. When you're hit with a case of last call surprise, you can either fake alcohol poisoning and bail or quickly usher the girl out of the bar and home with you before anyone's pupils adjust.

IN ORDER TO reduce the chances of last call surprise, if by 2 A.M. none of my leads are panning out, I'll start scrolling through my trusty cell phone address book to see what girls I can hit up late night. I use the latest technology in this endeavor. My phone has this great feature that lets me turn off my outgoing caller ID so that my number won't show up when I call someone that late. I call it the "booty call button."

A GROUP OF my fraternity brothers once took a trip to Prague in the Czech Republic. Out partying one night, they were dismayed to find the line to the bathroom was wrapped halfway around the bar. Cutting to the front of the line to get a closer look at the situation, my friends were surprised to see that the bathroom was not being used to its optimal capacity. While the confused Czechs looked on, my buddies entered the bathroom together

and all took a piss—one in the urinal, one
and one in the garbage can. The next day, t
city to go backpacking through Europe fo
Upon their return to Prague, they once again went out
to the local bar. After a few shots of absinthe, my friends
went to the bathroom, prepared to cut the long line
again. What they saw amazed them. The Czechs had
organized themselves into three short lines—one leading to the urinal, one to the sink, and one to the garbage can.

I ENJOY WATCHING old men at twentysomething bars
buy drinks for women who clearly aren't interested.
Because once they've plied these girls who are young
enough to be their daughters with enough alcohol, I can
move in and seal the deal easily and inexpensively. Hey,
who said hitting on chicks can't be both fun *and* afford-
able?

FOR SOME REASON, this year I suffered more RDIs
than at any time in my life. An RDI is of course a
"Random Drunken Injury" that you wake up with the
next day but have no idea how you got it. I've woken up
with a bruised tailbone, cut-up elbows, and sprained

.rists. And I don't know if I got them getting laid or laid out.

MAPQUEST NEVER WORKS quite the way you want it to, does it? It's like you hit zoom in once and you're looking at the bathroom of the bar and you hit zoom out and it shows you the continental United States. All I'm looking for is cross streets here.

HAVE YOU EVER been watching a new episode of *Saturday Night Live* and thought to yourself, wait a minute, what the fuck am I doing home right now?

EVER NOTICE THAT when you are with a bunch of guys approaching a bar, everyone instinctively slows up just before reaching the door? Or that half the time someone asks you for a bottle opener, they're holding a twist-off? Or that the more posh the club, the sloppier they allow you to dress? Or that every time you're about to go out, one of your buddies has to hold everyone up at the last minute to buy cigarettes and hit the ATM?

WHEN I PARTY, there's only one thing I'm more concerned with than how much tail is at the bar—it's deciding if and when to break the seal. Breaking the seal is of course a euphemism for taking your first piss of the night. Purely scientific studies done over many years in frat houses and other places of intoxication have proven that, as one participant put it, "Once you break the seal, you're fucked." Apparently, once initial urination takes place, the bladder is no longer capable of storage and instead becomes a conduit from the bottle of Amstel Light directly to the toilet (or sink if you happen to be in Prague).

DON'T YOU HATE when you're trying desperately to get a drink at a crowded bar and you finally get someone's attention and yell out your carefully scripted order, but then you realize it's just a busboy who happened to make eye contact but who has neither the authority nor the inclination to serve you anything?

BEFORE YOU TURN twenty-one, the last thing you want is to get ID'd at the bar. Once you turn twenty-one, you love getting ID'd at the bar. Then you turn twenty-three and you start getting annoyed when you're ID'd at the bar. When you're thirty, you again love getting ID'd at the bar. At twenty-five, I don't know if I should be insulted or flattered. I guess the more important question is, why have I been going to the same bar for five years?

IT DOES SEEM, though, that older people do remember clearly what it's like to be in your early twenties. I was at a bar once and some dancing drunk girl knocked into my arm, which caused me to jerk my hand up and chip a tooth on my Heineken. When I called my dentist's office the next day, I told the receptionist that I needed a chipped tooth fixed but didn't say how it happened. She looked at my chart, saw my date of birth, and said, "So, beer bottle, right?"

I'VE NOTICED A strange phenomenon among my friends as we get older: both our alcohol tolerance and the length of our hangovers are increasing. Never did I think that I would be able to hold more liquor now than I could in the dog days of college. It's quite a mystery. Of course, the side effect is that my hangovers are twice as brutal. My buddy Claudio got so bombed once, he actually threw up two days later. Now that's impressive.

MY OPINION OF a bar can change in about two seconds. Like when you're all excited about going to a particular bar and you motivate all your friends to go there . . . and then you get there and there's a huge line and they're not letting anyone in. All of a sudden you go from hyping the bar up to "This place sucks, who do they think they are, there's no way I am waiting on line for this shithole!"

MEMO TO DUDES wearing sports coats over T-shirts in bars: you're kidding me, right?

SOME OF THE many varieties of bars: the bar that you think you've never been to before, but then you walk in and you're like, "Oh, this place? I've been here ten times!" The bar that makes you wait on line outside forever, then you get in and the place is empty. The bar where you're like, "Wait, there's a downstairs? There's a whole other part of this place? Damn, I never knew that!" The bar where there are a hundred TVs showing sports highlights, making it incredibly difficult to maintain inane conversations with uninterested women. And lately I've been noticing bars that, once you are already inside, they make you wait on line and pay a cover again, just to get to the downstairs part, which you start to wish you never knew about in the first place.

BUT NO MATTER where you go, the worst about the bar is putting down a tab. Tabs kill me. Because once I put that credit card down, all of a sudden I become, "The most generous man who has ever lived!" "You guys want a drink? On my tab. You guys? Shots? On my tab. Ladies? Just put that on my tab, it's under Karo. You? Tab. You? Tab. Tab! Tab! Tab! Barkeep, bring me a round of your finest spirits, on my tab!" Then at the end of the night I get the bill and I'm like, "OK, who had a Miller Lite? You owe me four bucks. Seriously, pay up."

EVER TRY TO go somewhere "different?" You know, you try to go to a bar you haven't been to before and that won't be filled with your friends so you can meet new people. But what do you do when you get there? You strain your neck looking around for someone you know.

IS THERE ANYTHING more disgusting than when you're eating breakfast in your apartment the morning after having a bunch of people over to pre-game and you accidentally pick up a leftover screwdriver and drink it instead of your orange juice?

ALL GUYS KNOW that the most important attribute when determining whether or not to stay at a bar is the "Dude/Chick Ratio." The Dude/Chick Ratio can be determined upon entering a bar by scanning the crowd and simply taking count: "OK, let's see. Dude, chick, dude, dude, chick, dude, dude, chick, dude, dude, dude, dude, dude, dude . . . *dude*, let's get the fuck out of here!"

I DETEST AWKWARD moments—and there is nothing more awkward than not being introduced. I hate it when, by coincidence, I introduce two people who already know each other. They always make such a sarcastic show of it. "Oh, do I know Erica? Do I know Erica? Well, very nice to meet you, Erica! Karo, of course I know Erica, we went to school together!" Oh, sorry for being polite and thanks for making me feel so . . . well, awkward.

HOW COME WHENEVER I am introduced to people who are supposedly "so like me" I hate them?

I THINK THAT bars need to differentiate a little bit better between the male and female bathrooms. Quit trying to be so damn fancy. I walked over to the bathrooms at this bar the other night and looked at the illustrations on the two doors. One was like a cat with a top hat on and the other was a turtle in a tuxedo. Which one is male? I chose poorly.

AND WHEN WE leave the bathroom and then are immediately introduced to someone and shake their hand, do we really need to say, "Oh, it's only water" when referring to our wet hand? Isn't it safe to assume that if your hand is that wet, it's water? Maybe one time just for kicks I'll say, "Hey, nice to meet you. I'm Karo, and I just pissed all over myself."

I AM FASCINATED by bathroom attendants. To me, the sight of these people is proof that the economy is so bad we've been reduced to just making up jobs. Let's just say, for argument's sake, that I really do need baby powder, condoms, six kinds of cologne, and twenty different varieties of gum every time I use the bathroom. I certainly don't need all that stuff handed to me. And I definitely don't want to tip this guy every time I take a piss. It's like a urinal tollbooth in there.

IT REALLY BOTHERS me when bartenders give me back all singles. Listen, I understand the purpose is to encourage me to tip you, but giving me a wad of thirteen bills is not what I call good service.

EVERY TIME I take a break from New York nightlife to go on a binge-drinking, sun-soaked, tail-chasing vacation with my buddies, I end up getting sick exactly one week after we return home. I call this the "Acapulco Flu" because I first noticed the syndrome upon returning from Spring Break in college. When you're away, you barely eat or sleep but you're running on adrenaline the whole time so it doesn't affect you. But a week after you get back, your immune system decides *it* needs a vacation and suddenly you're on your deathbed. There is no known vaccination for the Acapulco Flu. Though not having a Bloody Mary as dinner six nights in a row probably helps.

I'LL NEVER FORGET the time I went to Miami and the hotel I was staying at was so hot you needed to be on a list to get a chair at the pool. There was a bouncer there with a clipboard and everything, even though we were guests at the hotel. The bouncer asked if we knew anyone so I did the only thing I could think of—I dropped my own name. It didn't work.

MARDI GRAS IS proof to me that mankind as a society and as a species has not evolved one bit in the past few thousand years. I've taken classes in negotiation at the world's most prestigious business school, but as soon as I hit Bourbon Street, I found myself ankle-deep in mud, beer, vomit, and trash, bartering with skanky women for a titty flash in exchange for a novelty necklace. For 72 hours straight. At the end of the weekend, I collapsed on a side street in exhaustion, partially asphyxiated under a crush of plastic beads and lit only by the dim glow of a passing *Girls Gone Wild* camera crew. I did learn one thing, though: any trip where you have to throw away your pants at the end is a good one.

I HATE DUDES wearing suits in bars (especially the guy on the cover of this book). Listen, buddy, it's a hundred degrees in here and no one is impressed that you're a fucking investment banker.

UNFORTUNATELY, IT SEEMS like most weekend nights are usually dedicated to celebrating people's birthdays.

Let's face it, there are about six people that you can really get excited for their birthdays and the rest of the people you just need to "make an appearance" at their party to perpetuate the thinly veiled fabrication that you actually care.

THERE IS ONE thing, though, that will prevent me from attending a birthday party, no matter who it's for: if they send me an Evite. Enough with the fucking Evites already! It's always the same drill: a picture of a martini glass in the background and directions to some bar in the West Village that no one has ever heard of. Then you have the guest list that is always some abnormally high number like 237 invited guests. Then you look at the "yes" section in which the first seven responses are the birthday girl's sister, roommates, cousins, and boyfriend, all with a little comment like "Wouldn't miss it for the world, baby doll!" Then you have the "maybe" section, also known as the "there's no fucking way I'm coming but I'm trying to be nice" section. Finally, there is the "no" section that usually consists of only a few scattered responses from friends in California or Europe who actually have a legitimate reason why they can't come. And just to punish the birthday girl for sending an Evite, no matter how detailed it was, the other 217 people who didn't respond always call up about half an hour before the party and say, "So what's the deal for tonight again?"

THERE HAVE BEEN some marked changes in the New York nightlife scene over the past few years. For instance, the new "in" spot at the bar is no longer the VIP room in the back or the tables near the front. No, the new "in" spot is actually outside the bar and around the corner, where flocks of hopelessly addicted chain-smokers huddle in deference to the wonderful new smoking ban. The landscape has changed such that by taking a brief cab ride down Park Avenue South, you can actually tell which lounges are most happening by the size of the nearby smoke cloud.

FORGIVE ME FOR venting here for a second. I fucking hate smokers. I hate smokers even more because they all whine about how expensive cigarettes are. Listen, no one wants to hear you bitch. I'm tired of smokers making lame-ass excuses why they don't quit. "Oh, I'm just a social smoker." "Dude, I had such a stressful day, I need a cigarette." "I only smoke when I'm drunk." Hey,

I only throw up on myself when I'm drunk but you don't see me getting any Camel bucks for that, do you? How dumb are you? You are fucking addicted! My eyes sting, my jacket is full of centimeter-sized circular holes, and the streets are dirty because of you. The smoking ban is a good start, but I'll be a lot happier once it starts snowing on all you fuckers.

THE OTHER DAY I felt like I was in camp or something. I had to write my name on the tag in my jacket before I went out. I love the art of trying to hide your jacket at the bar instead of checking it. You're wrapping it around bar stools, you're stuffing it behind couches, but no matter what happens, you always return four hours later to find it on the floor nowhere near where you put it with twenty-five identical jackets piled on top. It's like the lost and found at a J.Crew convention.

AFTER GIVING BIRTH, some women develop emotional problems. This is called "post-partum depression." After getting bombed, the next day I sometimes feel a little blue. I call this "post-party depression." One Sunday afternoon I was sitting on the couch hungover watching *Forrest Gump*, and I swear I almost broke down in tears.

NEXT TIME ONE of your buddies suggests an out-of-the-blue bar to go to one night, ask him if he got laid the last time he went there. As a rule, anyplace you go and get laid warrants a return visit, no matter how bad the place actually was.

ONE LITTLE PROBLEM I have is that, after a few dozen drinks, I tend to offend just about everyone in the bar. You know, now that I think about it, promoters and I have a lot more in common than I initially thought. After all, we both spend our weekend days communicating with partygoers via phone, email, and text message. The only difference is that promoters spend Saturday afternoon hyping up that evening's event to their friends and contacts, while I spend Sunday afternoon apologizing about the previous night to my friends and anyone else I had contact with.

THE "BALLS THEORY" is a corollary to the Dude/Chick Ratio I previously discussed. The Balls Theory goes like this: when going out with a group of guys to an exclusive club, your chances of getting in are inversely proportional to the amount of testicles present. If it's just me, I've got a 2:1 shot. If it's me and a friend, we've got a 4:1 shot. Four guys? An 8:1 shot, and so on. And that's the extent to which math will be used in this book from now on.

YOU HAVEN'T LIVED until you've drunkenly left your cell phone in a cab on a Saturday night. What usually follows is a three-hour odyssey in which you call your own phone about 3,000 times and pray that another passenger picks it up while simultaneously calling every cab company in the city to ask if by chance someone found a black Nokia until finally the cab driver calls you and says he'll bring you your phone if you pay him an extraordinary fee and, even though you are clearly being extorted by a crazed phone-hostage-taking madman, the very thought of waiting in line for two days at the cell phone store to get a replacement frightens you so much that you acquiesce to his demands and recover the phone before suffering the final humiliation of having to listen to 3,000 pathetic voice mails from yourself.

I HAVE ONE final nocturnal admission: I strongly feel you should never lie about your age to women at bars. Case in point: Triplet #1 and I were at this dive bar downtown that is frequented by NYU chicks. While I was distracted by the arcade game Golden Tee, Triplet #1 approached a bunch of cute girls and asked them if they went to NYU. They said they were first-years. Not wanting to intimidate a bunch of freshmen by telling them we were twenty-three, Triplet #1 lied and said we were juniors at NYU. When I joined the conversation I was then forced to continue the charade. As I talked to one of the girls, I slowly realized that something was terribly wrong. These chicks weren't freshmen at NYU, they were first-years at NYU Med. We had just lied ourselves younger than them. Fuck me!

FIVE

relative absurdity

When I was about a year old, my mom left me home with my dad for the whole day for the very first time. When she came home, she found my dad strangely quiet and me with a devious grin on my fat little face. Upon closer inspec-tion, my mom discovered that I was covered, head to toe, in a thin layer of white powder. She interrogated my dad, who broke pretty easily. After refusing to eat even a morsel of what my dad tried to feed me, I had forced him to give me powdered donuts for breakfast, lunch, and dinner. Thus, even as an infant, I knew how much my parents cared about me—and how to use it to my advantage.

Since I graduated and moved into my own place, I've had this urge to admit to my parents everything that

I did wrong or lied about in the past twenty-five years that they never caught. Like the time my dad's liquor went missing and I blamed it on the neighbors. Or when I came home half-drunk and vomiting on Mother's Day but blamed it on food poisoning. But, as I should have expected, instead of having a harmless laugh at my adolescent hijinks, my parents actually got retroactively upset about my transgressions. Thankfully, the statute of limitations on grounding has expired.

Even now, when I say that I'm going "home," I'm usually referring to my parent's house on Long Island, not my apartment in Manhattan. And even though if I wanted to, I could eat powdered donuts for breakfast, lunch, and dinner, I don't. I think that's telling. Family life obviously has a huge effect on who you become, an effect that does not diminish in your twenties, whether you like it or not. So in order for you to get to know me better, I'd like to take you inside the Karo family—a world of relative absurdity.

AFTER THE POWDERED donut incident, my early childhood remained fairly uneventful until that fateful evening in January 1982 when my parents brought home my newborn sister from the hospital. They carefully unwrapped her blankets, showed me her angelic face, and said, "Aaron, this is your new baby sister, Caryn." Upon hearing this, I immediately starting running around her crib yelling at the top of my lungs, "Caryn and Aaron! Caryn and Aaron! Caryn and Aaron!" My parents looked at each other in horror. Unwittingly, unknowingly, and inexplicably, they had somehow given their only two children rhyming first names.

SO I HAD to learn to survive in a cartoon family with an Aaron, a Caryn, and a cousin named Sharon. Imagine being ten years old, playing with your sister in the basement, and all you hear from upstairs is your mom yelling unintelligibly, "aaaaaaaaryn, come upstairs!" and having no idea whether she's calling you or your rhyming-name sister. To avoid confusion, friends started calling my sister Caryn and me Karo (pronounced *kay-roh*). And to this day, everyone I have ever met, from girlfriends to doormen, has always called me by my last name. I even insist that friends list me as Karo in their cell phones because Aaron usually comes first alphabetically and I end up getting a million calls from people dialing me by accident. Will the horror ever end?

I **ALWAYS ENJOY** when someone introduces me as Karo and the person looks at me quizzically and says, "Oh, um, what kind of name is that?" And I'm like, "Last."

LET'S TAKE A closer look at my parents. My mom, an education administrator whose job I only vaguely understand, is the kind of mom that, no matter where you are in the world, and no matter what's wrong with you, she's got some shit in her pocketbook that will make it better. "Mom, I skinned my knee." "Don't worry, honey, I have a Band-Aid in my purse." "Mom, I have a headache." "Don't worry, honey, I have some Advil in my purse." "Mom, we have a flat tire." "Don't worry, honey, I have a tire jack in my purse. Yeah, it's in the pocket with the zipper, next to the sugarless gum."

OF COURSE MY mom doesn't know her own cell phone number. I don't know why that is, but moms just don't know their own cell phone number. In fact, they usually have it written on an index card taped to the back of the phone. My mom also doesn't keep her cell phone on. She says it's only for emergencies. Well, how am I supposed to reach you in an emergency if your phone is off and stashed in that giant pocketbook of yours? But dads are just the opposite. Dads will pick up their cell phone no matter where they are and no matter what they're doing. My dad could be in the middle of open-heart surgery and he'll pick up the phone like, "Hey, sport, I'm in the middle of an operation but I saw you on Caller ID and just wanted to make sure everything was OK." Which is weird, because my dad's not even a doctor.

MY DAD, WHO is a toy company executive by weekday and a golf-playing, golf magazine-reading, golf-on-TV-watching, golf school-attending fanatic on the weekends, has always taught me about the important things in life. My senior year in high school, he attended parent-teacher conferences. When he met with my biology teacher, he noticed pictures on the wall of everyone in the class at a field trip we had taken a few weeks earlier. Pictures of everyone except for me. When he came home, he told me we had to talk. I was scared out of my mind. He asked me why I missed the school field trip. I said to him, "Dad, I have to level with you. I cut school that day and took the train to the city to watch the Yankees World Series victory parade." I'll never forget his response. "Son," he said, "This is the proudest moment of my life."

AS YOU CAN see, I'm a diehard Yankees fan going back many generations. In fact, my family is no longer allowed to watch movies starring fellow Yankees fan Billy Crystal because my dad is still mad at him for wearing a Mets hat in *City Slickers*.

MY SISTER, CARYN, who is two and a half years younger than me, has suffered from the classic second-child disadvantages. While shelves full of albums and scrapbooks document my early years (including a pouch with some hair from my first haircut), my sister's history was relegated to a couple of Polaroids and an old coloring book. Despite this checkered past, my sister will forever remain the Good One in the family. Though we have both been very successful in our lives, Caryn is sweet, caring, and interested in helping others, whereas I am loud, obnoxious, and selfish. I just can't win.

I AM IN my early twenties, but whenever I fly anywhere, I have to send my parents an itinerary with flight numbers and times. And call them as soon as I land. Even layovers.

AND WHEN YOU leave the state to go somewhere, do your parents suggest you visit relatives who really don't live anywhere near where you're going? I called my mom to tell her I was going to Detroit to visit some of my fraternity brothers. She was like, "Oh, you should visit your cousin Rob!" I'm like, "Cousin Rob lives in New Orleans. Just because I'm going to be in the airport doesn't mean I can go visit him!"

MY DAD LOVES the duty-free shop. There's just something about duty that gets him all worked up. On every family vacation we took when we were little kids, all I remember is filling up Caryn's stroller with half-price bottles of Absolut.

EVER NOTICE THAT dads carry more in their pockets than any humans on earth? My dad turns a pair of khaki shorts into an overnight bag.

MY MOM HAS almost superhero-like powers. You tell her what time a movie is playing, how long it's been out, and how many stars it got, and she'll tell you to the minute when you have to leave the house in order to get to the theater before it sells out. Then she'll come with you and make you sit through the entire credits at the end because she wants "to see who that guy with the shirt was."

BUT LIKE ANY superhero, my mom has weaknesses. Her Kryptonite is cameras. She's had the same one for three years and still can't work it. My family went to Scotland to visit my sister who was studying abroad. My dad played St. Andrews, the oldest golf course in the world, in the middle of a monsoon. When he stepped back into the clubhouse, he was soaked to the bone and carrying his clubs with tears in his eyes. My mom was ready for this once-in-a-lifetime shot . . . and couldn't figure out to work the flash. Thankfully, I was prepared for such a scenario and snapped the picture with a disposable. And that's what family is all about.

MY MOM IS always "finishing the roll." Her camera has 27 pictures, she's only taken fifteen of them, but she really wants to get them developed, so she's snapping pictures of the kitchen, the front door of our house, the lawn, our neighbors' car. In all of our family albums half the pictures are of us and the other half are of assorted inanimate objects.

WHEN IT COMES to the phone, my mom sure has a knack for timing. Like when she calls me at noon on a Saturday and asks what I'm doing that night. I'm like, Mom, I haven't even started my hangover yet, how could I possibly know what I'm doing tonight? Then there was the time when I was having a lot of trouble sleeping. My mom looked up some tips on the Internet and called me on her way to work to tell me about them—thereby waking me up at eight in the morning.

NOTHING KILLS GOOD news like having to tell the same story over the phone to your dad and then your mom consecutively. Because once you get to your mom, you're already pissed that she didn't pick up the other phone and listen to the story the first time so you give her the abridged version, which she can't follow. Then you have to go all the way back to the beginning and remind her who each person in the story is. And by the time you're through, you hope you never have good news again. But at least that's better than when you tell your dad a story, he relays it your mom, and then she calls you the next day to ask about it and couldn't have gotten the facts more wrong. It's like a fucked up game of telephone but there are only three people in the chain.

AND WHEN YOU'RE telling your parents a story, do you find yourself giving your friends little nicknames to help jog your parent's memory, because otherwise they'll have no idea who the hell you're talking about? My parents ask me who I went out with last night and I'm like, well, there was law school Jason, Giants tickets Jeff, lazy eye Steve, '92 Nissan Altima Lisa, and her boyfriend, you remember him, we went out to dinner once, you know, medium rare porterhouse with a side of creamed spinach Trevor? And they actually do.

BUT THE ALL-TIME worst is when your parents call you on a Saturday night, but you've already gone out so you don't get the message until later when you're drunk and it freaks you out. Because no matter what the message says, it is always vague enough to get you all worried so that you can't enjoy the rest of the night until you make sure no one died. Of course, your mom's cell phone is off in her gigantic pocketbook and when you finally get a hold of her after trying desperately for an hour she says, "Oh, honey, I didn't mean to worry you, I just knew you were coming home tomorrow and it's going to be chilly, so don't forget a jacket." Are you serious, Mom?

HAVE YOUR PARENTS reached that age where they're still employed but don't really seem to work anymore? It seems like my parents are constantly taking days off with no explanation other than they felt like it. It's like they're taking early retirement . . . early.

MY COUSIN RECENTLY had a baby. Objectively speaking, Daniel is the cutest baby of all time. The thing is, when your cousin has a baby, you don't become anything cool like an uncle or something. In fact, now I'm a second cousin. It's like I got demoted.

IT'S PRETTY AMAZING to me, but my sister, Caryn, can actually tell which episode of *Friends* is on by watching only the first six seconds of the show. The credits will roll, Phoebe will walk in the room, and before she even says anything, my sister is like, "This is the one where

Joey's tailor molests him!" And this is why my family likes her better than me?

MY MOM HAS the same two responses to everything that I complain about. She either says, "You drink too much" or "Open a window." I'll say, "Mom, I don't feel so well." "You drink too much." "But Mom, I didn't have anything to drink." "Then open a window." "Mom, the landlord just called and he's going to raise my rent but I can't afford it." "You know why you can't afford it—you drink too much." "Mom, I just found out my friend is getting engaged—I'm freaking out, they just met, it's not going to work out and—" "OK, just calm down, relax, open a window." "Mom, I'm looking after my neighbor's three-year-old and this girl is driving me crazy, she's running around, I don't know what's wrong with her!" "You know what the problem is, *she* drinks too much."

WHEN I'M IN my apartment just hanging out or watching TV, a lot of times I'll crack open a beer. This wasn't always the case. In high school, I hated the taste of beer. In college, I said I loved it but still didn't really like it that much. Now, I can honestly say sitting on the couch and drinking a beer is one of my favorite activities. Of course, to my mom, this is the worst development in my life since I told her I had a fake ID. She's always been like, "Aaron, why can't you just nurse one beer?" Now I can finally say, "Mom, I am nursing just one beer." It just happens to be at 7 P.M. on a Tuesday for no reason.

AREN'T PARENTS JUST adorable? The tiniest little things make them happy. My mom got a new cell phone and I changed the greeting on the main screen from "Verizon" to "Supermom." Considering that her mastery of this device is limited to dialing my number and hitting the key with the picture of the green phone on it, I won like a thousand good son points.

YOU WANT TO know what the easiest way to confuse my parents is? I send them an email . . . with an attachment. All hell breaks loose. "Aaron, what did you send me? What is this? What do I do? Do I right click the paper-clippy thing? What is this? What do I do?" I'm always like, "Mom, you drink too much!"

MUCH TO MY father's chagrin, another summer has passed without my taking up golf. I try to explain to him that it's not that I don't like the sport itself, it's just that it involves two of my least favorite activities: getting up early and being outside when it's hot.

THERE IS A tradition in the Karo family that when you graduate from college and get your first real job and your first real paycheck, you have to take the entire family out to a really nice dinner. My dad has been holding this dinner over my head for as long as I can remember. After I graduated from Penn, I finally got to take the family out. Of course, since I was picking up the tab, my dad ordered like lobster-encrusted filet mignon. You should have seen my dad's face when I signed the bill. Actually, you can. He had the waiter take a picture.

MY SISTER, IN continuing her devious quest to one-up me, recently graduated from Dartmouth. While driving home after the ceremony, I asked my parents how they felt about giving birth to two Ivy League graduates. My mom's response: "Proud." My dad's: "Poor."

I AM THE last male Karo in my family. Therefore, it is up to me to carry on the Karo name. My grandma has been holding this over my head forever. She always tells me that I absolutely must have four boys to carry on the Karo name. "Four boys! You gotta give me four boys!" is all she ever says. No pressure or anything, Grandma. She started making me promise her four boys when I was like six years old. I didn't even like girls yet!

AS YOU CAN see, the Karo family is quirky and crazy, but full of love. Everything I've accomplished I owe to them. But if I ever actually have four sons, you can bet your ass they won't have rhyming names. I was recently reminded just how relatively absurd my family really is when my dad went on a diet and lost a lot of weight. I'm very proud of him and he looks great. The only problem I have with the whole thing is that it seems as if all family members are now required to comment on his weight loss each and every time we see him, even if you've already commended him. Otherwise, my dad gets offended. So now I've had to rack my brain every time I come home in order to come up with a new compliment on his trim figure. Last time I visited, I decided I'd had enough and didn't say anything. Sure enough, my dad gave me a hard time. When I complained to my mom about it, you know what she said? "Open a window." Fuck me.

SIX

job insecurity

The other day, I found myself sitting on the couch watching reruns of *Lizzie McGuire* on the Disney Channel (and feeling sort of guilty because I was kinda getting turned on). And as I began to doze off, I realized something—I hadn't worked full-time in over two years. Now don't get me wrong, upon graduation I did the right thing and took a fancy job on Wall Street. I lasted about thirteen months.

In the past decade, there have only been two times when I shaved my sideburns off completely. One was after my first night of pledging when my pledgemaster told me that if I didn't shave them off, he would. The other was after my first day of work when I was told that facial hair was "frowned upon" in the office. In both cases, I grew them back without anyone noticing, was summarily shit upon for months on end for no apparent reason, and when it was all over, had learned nothing more than a few bizarre and mundane skills not applicable anywhere else.

The plight of the twentysomething in corporate America is a paradoxical one. We don't want jobs but need them to pay our obscene rent. We hate our jobs but are scared to death of losing them. We spend most of our time on the job searching for new, exciting jobs, only to find out they suck just as badly as the last one. We've entered the era of job insecurity.

Despite thoroughly enjoying my second career as a comedian, my time on Wall Street blessed me with experience and perspective, and allowed me to sock some money away to support my current gluttonous lifestyle. However, I am frightfully aware that my new career is tenuous. One day, I just might return to the cold, harsh reality of the working world. But this time, I'm keeping the sideburns.

NO MATTER WHAT they do for a living, every twentysomething in the country has the same priority as soon as they get home from work: get undressed as soon as possible. I used to go from three-piece suit to boxers and dress socks in under six seconds flat.

GETTING UP AT the crack of dawn for work is sort of like doing the *New York Times* crossword puzzle—it gets harder and harder as the week goes on until it's almost impossible on Friday. And when your alarm goes off and you sit up in bed with one eye open, you always do that silent "reverse acceptance speech" where you curse every person of authority in your life. You think to yourself, I'd like to say that I hate everyone who brought me to this moment at 5:45 A.M. I hate my parents, my boss, and, of course, my co-workers who come out every single day to support me. I hate you all. And now I'm going to snooze for seven more minutes. Good night. Assholes.

WHY DO GIRLS carry that extra bag to work? Everyone's got their laptop bag and maybe their gym bag, but girls always have that extra Bath & Body Works shopping bag piled high with crap. Is there something they're not telling us?

IN OUR FIRST jobs out of college, we are so naive. We don't realize that being given a pager, cell phone, or

BlackBerry by our company is very, very bad. Sure, the NYU chicks at the bar may think it's cool when you pull that little toy out of the holster on your belt to send a quick email, but everyone else just thinks you're a jackass. Plus, now your boss can find you wherever you go. You know what other organization has that capability? Prison. I do not believe this is a coincidence.

YOUR FIRST DRUG test is a rite of passage in corporate America that all twentysomethings remember. I'll never forget mine. Most people in line for the bathroom were calm and collected while everyone who partied in college was cowering in the back and chugging huge bottles of Poland Spring. While peeing in the cup, my buddy Harlan suddenly realized he had more business to take care of in the bathroom. So he calmly turned around and took a dump while the rest of the puzzled first-years waited patiently outside the single stall. Now that's stickin' it to the Man!

THE FIRST THING I would do as soon as I got to work Monday morning, after checking my email, eating a bagel, going to the bathroom, thoroughly browsing ESPN.com and CNN.com, and checking my email again, was turn to my buddy in the adjacent cubicle and start making plans for Friday night. Surprisingly, by the time Friday actually came around, we still didn't have any concrete plans. It's always nice, though, to have someone at work that you also hang out with socially. That way when you leave the office there's someone to commiserate with about how much you want to kill your male co-workers and bone the female ones.

SOME OF MY friends belong to corporate softball leagues and play with their co-workers several times a week. Sometimes I wish I was part of something like that, because I'm a very competitive person and there's nothing really for me to compete for anymore. The last time I played semi-organized athletics was my Greek League soccer team in college. My fraternity made it all the way to the finals but when the championship game was scheduled for a Thursday night at 9 P.M., we forfeited and went out drinking instead.

WHY IS IT that office-organized athletic events always end with mass consumption of food and/or alcohol? It's not enough to play in the corporate softball league or participate in a charity run through Central Park with your co-workers. Afterward, you must go out with the team to consume large amounts of fatty foods and dark beer, thus impairing your judgment until you wax enthusiastic about the office and neutralizing the effects of any of the mildly aerobic activity you just completed.

THE NEXT TIME I'm in an office elevator that keeps making stops and someone jokes, "Hey, must be the local!" I'm gonna punch him in the neck.

THERE ARE FEW things worse than attempting to make it through a day of work with a massive hangover. You know, you're perspiring slightly, you have a huge glass of ice water, you're trying to stay very, very still, you tell everyone you have food poisoning, it's horrible. I actually threw up in the office once. I came back from the bathroom and everyone was giving me a dirty look. I told them that I had some bad sushi and they all just shook their heads and went back to work. The funny thing is that I really did have some bad sushi the night before. Plus twenty sake bombs.

RIGHT UP THERE with trying to survive when you're

hungover in the office is trying to stay awake at your desk after you come back from lunch. It should really be an Olympic sport. It's a beautiful day out, you just went out to eat and had a nice turkey sandwich, then you get back to your desk and all of a sudden you become narcoleptic. Phones are ringing off the hook, people are yelling, but your Herman Miller chair is the most comfortable bed in the world. I once fell asleep for so long on my computer that when I woke up I had impressions from the *F* and *J* keys in my forehead.

NEXT TIME I see one of my friends use his middle initial on a business card or email signature, I'm gonna kick his ass. What are you, forty years old?

I LOVE CORPORATE America's futile attempts at boosting employee morale. For instance, the Friday afternoon beer bash. Have you participated in one of these? You get to stop work early on Friday and hang out in a drafty conference room sipping lukewarm Heinekens with a bunch of co-workers you already spend twelve hours a day with. Um, yeah . . . could I, uh, just go home early instead? Because that would really make me a lot happier.

ONCE I ATTENDED a Friday afternoon beer bash at an actual bar. We even got bracelets that entitled us to free alcohol. So I made some small talk and chugged a few cocktails on the house, then got the hell out of there and headed to a different bar downtown to meet my buddies. Coincidentally, at the second bar, another company was having a Friday afternoon beer bash for its own disgruntled first-years. But here's the best part—the bracelet they were using happened to be identical to mine so I drank for free again! And for one night at least, I was King.

SOMETIMES IT SEEMS like every one of my friends has become an investment banker. Now, if you've never worked in an investment bank, you may be fooled into thinking this is a glamorous and sophisticated job. It's not. I'm going to let you in on a little secret. If you're under twenty-five and work anywhere in an investment bank, this is what you do all day: copy and paste numbers from one Excel spreadsheet to another, proofread, spell check and page number documents, and fudge expense reports to enable you and your friends to eat as much free food as possible. For 90 hours a week.

ONE AFTERNOON, MY friend Adam, a typical disgruntled investment banker, was going out to lunch with a few co-workers, all wearing the standard blue J.Crew shirt, gray Banana Republic pants, and black Kenneth Cole shoes. A cheerful secretary passed the weary group in the hall and said, "Hey, you guys all look the same!" To which Adam replied, "You mean miserable?"

WHEN YOU CALL an investment banker, I think you can judge how disgruntled he is by the length of the sigh he makes after he picks up the phone but before he starts talking.

I THINK THE most important skill that any twentysomething working in an office must learn is how to look busy when you're really not. The easiest way to do this, of course, is to throw a bunch of paper around your desk to make it look really messy and keep a complicated-looking document up on your computer screen. And how do you know when you've been pretending to look busy in the office for too long? When you reach that moment—and I know you have—when you decide that you've officially surfed every web site on the entire Internet (including AaronKaro.com) and have been reduced to Googling yourself. At that point, you should probably make sure you're actually still employed.

EVER TRY TO explain to your grandmother what you do for a living? No matter what you do, it's always way too complicated to explain. You're like, well, you see, our clients are looking to raise additional capital and we provide a liquid market for . . . uh, yeah, you're not following this. How about this? I'm a stockbroker. Yup, just like on TV.

I HATE WHEN I call my friends at work and an assistant picks up and says, "Mr. Smith's office!" Can you give me a fucking break, please? Mister? I know you don't have an office. I also know that same assistant answers the phone for a dozen other drones. In fact, I bet she has a bigger cubicle than you do. So get off your lazy ass and pick up your own damn phone because now the assistant wants to know what I'm calling "in regards to." She won't transfer me unless I tell her what this is "in regards to," even though there's no regards! Finally, I just get fed up and say, "Do you really want to know what this is in regards to? Do you really want to know? Well, I'm calling to ask if *Mr.* Smith got head from that chick we met last night, OK?" And I get transferred right away.

AFTER A YEAR or two of mind-numbing tedium, when you've convinced yourself that there's got to be a better cubicle out there somewhere, you clandestinely start putting together your resume. Writing your resume boils down to one thing: making the dumbass shit you do sound impressive. "Did" becomes "utilized," "helped" becomes "facilitated," "boss's dry cleaning" becomes "value-added relationship management." I used to love reading the resumes of frat boys like myself because I knew that "fraternity treasurer" really means "in charge of beer purchasing and money laundering."

AFTER YOU'VE ADJUSTED the margins on your resume for the twentieth time and have finally sent it out and gone on interview after interview, nothing is worse than waiting for "them" to get back to you. Ask any job-seeking twentysomething how their search is going and they'll invariably tell you the same thing: "I think I'm pretty close to getting something, I'm just waiting for them to get back to me." I hate "them." "Them" cowers behind an anonymous assistant every time you call.

"Them" makes you endure the cruel and unusual process of interviewing for a job without knowing how much it pays. "Them" is leading you on even though "them's" niece has the position all locked up. You know what I say? Fuck "them."

EVEN WORSE IS when you are told by a prospective employer that they don't have any openings but that they'll keep your resume on file. I just want to know one thing—where the fuck is this file? It must have about a million resumes in it at this point. And let's be honest, is there any chance that a resume will get plucked from there and someone gets a job? Doubtful. "We'll keep your resume on file" is just another way of saying, "Please stop calling, we hired a chimpanzee instead."

MANY OF MY friends spend more time in the office looking for a different job than actually doing work. The secretive nature of searching for a new job while still at your old job means that when your friends call, you can't just give them an update because you don't want your boss to hear that you're about to jump ship. I've actually become quite adept at discerning what the hell my buddy at work is trying to tell me about his meeting with a headhunter by using a few benign code words and a lot of yes or no questions. It's like playing white-collar Taboo.

SINCE SOME OF my friends are now moving on to their second job since leaving college, I've been asked a few times to write letters of recommendation for them. It always goes something like this: "Hey, Karo, I was wondering if you could write a letter about me for this new job I'm trying to get. Here's the thing, don't mention anything about that time I almost burned down the fraternity house. Or punched that cop. Or stole that car. Or that I failed Accounting. Or that I never actually graduated. Or that I'm functionally illiterate." I'm like, sure, no problem, one complete lie coming up!

NOTHING MAKES MY day like receiving a corporate farewell email. After "them" finally gives your co-worker a new job and when he's done taking down all his Dilbert cartoons and stealing ballpoint pens, the only thing left to do before leaving is write a mass good-bye email. Through thinly veiled euphemisms like "incredible learning experience," "keep in touch," and "warm regards," you can almost feel the undeniable hatred toward everyone in the office. And of course you write back "Good luck!" which really means, "I never liked you anyway!"

HOW COME WHEN you quit a job you have to give two weeks notice but when they lay you off you have to leave immediately?

THE END OF the year brings with it one of our most joyous of traditions—the office holiday party. You've got to love a society where every year we gather to celebrate record-low profit margins and the opportunity to fuck inebriated co-workers. I always enjoyed standing on the outskirts of the dance floor with my fellow entry-level grunts, blue button-downs rolled up at the sleeves and an Amstel in each hand. The key was to find any female employee who seemed to be dancing excessively. Because that, in our Neanderthal minds, meant she was easy. It's amazing Wall Street doesn't just collapse upon itself in stupidity. More often, anyway.

THE "OFF-SITE" MEETING is another misdirected attempt to boost productivity. Ostensibly, the purpose of the off-site is to gather the whole team in a mildewed conference room somewhere far from the actual office to prevent distraction and engage in embarrassing team-building exercises. In reality, everyone spends half the day in the hallway checking their voice mail and about the only team-building that occurs is the unanimous agreement that the sandwiches brought in for lunch are soggy and inedible.

IT IS A sad fact that many women I know tell me they get harassed at work on a daily basis by disgusting guys. Now I'm not talking blatant breast-touching or the "date me or I'll fire you" type of harassment, I'm talking about subtle, constant, inappropriate emails and innuendos from ugly, balding, married men. I'm pretty ashamed of my own gender for this. Crude and improper behavior belongs in the bar, not the boardroom, guys!

LET'S FACE IT, the working world is full of annoying people. Here are some of my least favorite. Men who have female assistants leave their outgoing voice mail message. People who leave their outgoing voice mail message in such a hushed tone that you can barely hear what the hell they're saying. People who change their outgoing voice mail message when they go on vacation but then forget to change it back for a month after they return. People who bombard me with mass emails containing "new contact info" when I never contact them in the first place. People who have an underscore in their email address. People who don't save their documents regularly and lose all their work every time their computer crashes. People who keep a tube of toothpaste in their desk so that they can brush their teeth every time they touch a morsel of food. People who take the elevator only one floor. People who wear sneakers to work and then change into shoes when they get there. People who proudly wear their employee ID card around their neck all day long and refuse to take it off. Guys who would rather wear a suit than be business casual. And, finally, unnecessary business-card-exchangers who force their card upon you at the bar even though you have no fathomable use for their services nor any desire to contact them in the foreseeable future.

ONE SIDE EFFECT of being a cog in the system at work is that you no longer feel remorse about lying. In fact, you are encouraged to lie, on the job and about your job. Only in corporate America, it's called "recruiting." I'm sure in college you attended at least one job fair where you were regaled with bullshit tales of corporate wonder by an employee who only months earlier stood in your shoes getting lied to himself. No wonder one of my buddies had no qualms about sticking a dozen cotton balls in his mouth once so that he could call his boss and pretend he just had his wisdom teeth out and couldn't come to work.

YOU CAN USUALLY tell if the company you work for is a legitimate, money-making enterprise or little more than a chop shop by whether or not the firm offers "Summer Fridays." Summer Fridays is a strange policy in which employees get a half day or even a full day off every Friday from Memorial Day to Labor Day. Whatever CEO came up with giving his workforce 20% of the summer off as a paid vacation surely gained him the admiration of his employees and disdain of his shareholders. Of course, I never enjoyed Summer Fridays. Instead we were offered an even bolder perk. During the summer months we were—brace yourself— allowed to wear khakis. Oh boy.

JUST ONCE, WHEN you're walking down the hallway at work and a co-worker is walking toward you and you both almost walk right into each other because you both moved the same way and then you laugh under your breath and start sort of stutter-stepping to try to get around one another, don't you just want to uppercut the guy in the face and be done with it already?

DO YOU TELL your boss when you're leaving for the day? That's always a dilemma, right? You don't want to draw too much attention to the fact that you're leaving nor create a precedent where you have to tell him or her that you're leaving every day. The best bet is usually to wait until your boss leaves before taking off yourself—about 90 seconds later.

ANYONE READING THIS right now knows that there is one thing about work that is worse than everything else combined. Taking a shit in the office. I know, I know, with the economy in shambles and sexual harassment running rampant, this should be the least of our concerns. But it's not. Shitting at the office is akin to desecrating our most sacred ritual. The primary issue is the noise factor. Solution? Time your thrusts to coincide with co-workers' coughs and sink usage. Then there is the uncertainty principle. Don't go into a stall if you see the person who just came out. You never want to match a face to an ass. You can also use the bathroom on a different floor. Even though the architectural layout is bound to be identical, the fact that you won't be able to recognize anyone's shoes is somehow comforting. Of course, if you're really shit-shy, you can always use the bathroom they use for drug tests. My friend Harlan says it's quite roomy.

I WORKED IN an office with some of the smartest young minds in the business. Graduates of Harvard, Duke, and Amherst. And no one could work the fax machine. In fact, I would venture to say that the most difficult aspects of working on Wall Street are faxing and printing. Once, I was late for a meeting when the printer broke for the sixth time that week. The error message said, "Load magenta toner." I almost broke down in tears when I realized that I had graduated from Wharton yet only understood one out of three words in the message.

THE BUSINESS TRIP, like the BlackBerry, is another corporate mirage. Sure, it sounds cool to your mom that you're going on an all-expenses paid trip to Dallas, but let's face it, if you're under twenty-five and going on a business trip, all you pretty much get to see is the airport, a Starbucks, a mildewed conference room eerily similar to the one where you had your last off-site, the hotel, one fancy steakhouse, and then the airport again. All within 24 hours.

HAVE YOU EVER been so bored at work that you contemplated asking for more work to do, then when you got more work instantaneously regretted opening your big, stupid mouth in the first place? Ever ask someone you just met where they work and they say, "Thirtieth and Park" like you actually wanted to know their office's physical location instead of what company they work for? Ever notice that no matter what the temperature in the office is, the women always think it's too cold and are bundled up in sweaters while the men think it's too hot and are sweating profusely? And ever notice that no matter what he's wearing, whenever you see a co-worker outside of the office in casual clothes, he always looks just a little off?

PERFORMING TEDIOUS TASKS at work is like studying for finals in college because you stop to check your email every two minutes even though there's no way you have any new messages. I guess the only difference is that finals only last two weeks and you'll be working for the next forty years. Wow, that's depressing.

I HATE IT when people in the office try to be nice and they hold the door open for you when you're still like fifty feet away and you have to do that little racewalk in order to get to the door faster and you just wish they wouldn't try to be so nice in the first place.

HAVE YOU EVER noticed that no one has any idea how to use the conference call feature on their phone at work? You'll be talking to a buddy and say, "Hey, why don't we get Brad on the phone?" And your friend will fiddle around for a minute and then say, "Hold on," put the phone on his shoulder, lean back in his chair, peer out of his cubicle, and shout, "Hey, does anyone know how to use conference on these phones?"

I THINK EVERYONE has that friend who no one knows what he does for a living. You ask someone and they'll be like, "Yeah, he was dabbling a bit here and there and then he got this new job but the company went out of business so then he went to work for his dad but he quit that and now he's doing a little thing on the side while he studies for his LSATs." Figures. You know what I call the LSATs? The get-out-of-life-free card.

EVER GET AN email from a friend at work who is trying to outwit the system that scans all of his outgoing messages? It's always something like: "Hey, Karo, what the f@ck happened with that b_tch last night? Her t*its were huge! I want all the details, you m%ther f@cker!" I'm like, are you sure your company won't be able to figure this out?

I LOVE READING the automatic disclaimers at the end of emails coming from employees of major corporations. It's always something like, "Nothing in this email can be construed as an offer to buy or sell anything. The person sending this email cannot and will not be trusted. We make no guarantee that we even know the person sending this email. We make no guarantee that the person who sent this email is even the person who wrote this email, but either way, we do not know him, her, it, or them. We are not responsible for anything that has happened in the past, is happening now, might happen, or will happen anywhere in the universe until the end of time. If this message was sent to you in error, please destroy your computer and kill everyone around you. Thank you."

HAVE YOU EVER been working on the computer and a little warning window pops up when you do something? Usually under the warning there is a box you can check that says, "Never show me this message again." I always think to myself—never? *Never?* I don't know, that's a pretty big commitment to make. I think I'll keep it around just in case.

EVERY TWENTYSOMETHING HATES being the low rung on the totem pole in the office and vows to remember that feeling when they reach a position of power. Until the summer interns come and you immediately make one your personal bitch. Really, the office is just one big fraternity. You start off as the lowly pledge wishing death upon your boss, the pledgemaster. But as soon as you get a taste of his power, you fail to remember all about your own experience and hope that the first-years fear you. It's amazing how quickly we forget what it feels like to shave our sideburns.

FOR ME, THE moment I knew I was spending too much time in the office was when I caught myself using buzzwords with my family. I was like, "Hey, Mom, just as an FYI, I touched base with Dad earlier. Yeah, he's out of pocket right now but we're gonna circle back in about an hour. I really think it's critical that he gives us the view from 50,000 feet because there seems to be some disconnect between . . . wait a minute, what the fuck am I talking about?"

WHEN YOU DO decide to leave a job, I say do it in style, like take all your vacation days in a row and then never show up again. For me, my guilty pleasure on the way out was to grab a huge stack of personalized pads with my name and the company logo on it. In hindsight, though, I'm not really sure who else would want them, but I actually still use those pads to this day to write down jokes. Some people work on Wall Street for the experience, power, and money, but not me. I did it for the stationery.

IN THE END, I don't think I was cut out for Wall Street. My three least favorite things in life are waking up early, shaving, and tucking in my shirt. Obviously, I chose the wrong profession. Now that I think about it, being a twentysomething in the era of job insecurity really all comes down to one thing—being tucked in. When you're working, you have to tuck in your shirt. You're stuffy, you're uncomfortable, and your crotch itches. When you're out of the office, you're untucked—you're loose, free, and uninhibited. I don't think we were meant to spend our early twenties, our most cherished years, all tucked in. It's not natural. I do realize, though, that not everyone has the luxury of leaving their steady job and becoming a comedian. But just remember, the only one in the office looking out for you, is you. For example, one gloomy afternoon, as I roamed the thirtieth floor of my company's mammoth skyscraper, I came across a desolate and sparsely decorated cubicle. Sitting on the desk between an unused monitor glare guard and an ergonomic mouse pad was the book *Don't Sweat the Small Stuff at Work.* Half absentmindedly, I picked up the book and found that I was soon heartened by its spirited tales of teamwork and levity in the workplace. I turned to a nearby receptionist and asked whose cubicle I was standing at. Eyeing the book in my hand, she replied, "Oh, you can just take that, he was laid off last week." Fuck me.

SEVEN

fat, broke & hungry

As I wrote in *Ruminations on College Life,* when I stepped down from the podium after delivering a speech at graduation, I spotted my parents in the crowd. I saw the huge smile on my mom's face and tears coming from my dad's eyes, and that's when I knew it was all over. They would never give me money ever again. In the weeks that followed, financial independence was thrust upon me. My parent's credit cards were cut in half, our joint bank accounts were closed, and (gasp!) I even opened a 401(k), all under the watchful eye and satisfied grin of my father.

Like most twentysomethings, the complete fulfillment of all my wildest desires and fantasies is held back only by insufficient funds. Maybe it's because my spending is so erratic. Like how come I regularly use my expired college ID to get a dollar off of a meal at Subway but refuse to use coupons? I also think my wallet is bulimic. I binge all week, saving up and not spending much, and then on the weekend I purge, throwing away fistfuls of cash at a time in exchange for watered-down drinks and imported beer. By the end of the weekend, I'm poor and cleaning up my own puke.

I also spend way too much money on food. This wouldn't be a problem if take-out in this city weren't so damn expensive. When did everything become pan-Asian, Asian-fusion, or tapas? What the fuck happened to cheeseburgers? And whatever money is left after I engorge myself goes to pay the dues at my fancy gym where I vainly attempt to work off everything I just consumed. If you think about it, the life and times of twentysomethings really revolve around figuring out how to satiate our stomachs and flatten our abs without doing too much damage to our wallets. It's a vicious cycle that usually leaves me feeling fat, broke, and hungry.

I'M CONVINCED THAT virtually the only thing I spend my money on is alcohol. I get my credit card bill back and it breaks down all my charges by category. I usually only have one category listed: "Food & Drink." The thing reads like a *Zagat* guide to New York bars.

IT'S WEIRD BECAUSE now that I'm on my own, and it's my own money, I spend a lot more freely than I did when it was my parent's money. I guess before I felt kind of bad if I dropped a hundred bucks of my mom's money at the bar. Now I don't feel bad at all because the only person I have to answer to is myself. And he's usually too drunk to care anyway.

ONE OF THE most depressing experiences in twentysomething life is having to go to the ATM two days in a row. And each time, even though you don't have any money for anyone to steal, you try to shield your pin code from other people. But you don't want to look all paranoid so you do that subtle little elbow move to try to block people from looking. Sometimes, I'll even pretend like I am going to press the number five, but then at the very last second, I'll actually press four. That really seems to throw people off.

AFTER-HOURS ATM centers can be quite awkward. These are the places that you can swipe your card at any time and go into a little building where you can use the ATM. When you're in there, someone always comes to the door and stands there because their card isn't swiping right and they can't get in. So you have to decide in like five seconds whether this person is actually an upstanding citizen whose card isn't working right or a vicious killer who is going to rob then murder you. Of course, no one wants to be rude, so I end up pretty much letting everyone in. But I definitely make sure to do my elbow move so the murderer won't get my pin number before he kills me!

ATM FEES POSE a conundrum for many: "Wait a minute, I have to pay money just to get money?" My buddy Claudio is so morally opposed to paying ATM fees that whenever he needs cash he hops on the subway to his bank downtown. Cost of a round-trip subway fare? $4.00. ATM fee he is trying to avoid? $1.50. Having a friend that's a fucking idiot? Priceless.

I WAS PRETTY proud of myself when I signed up for my first credit card. Until I caught a glimpse of my dad's wallet. He has 187 different credit cards. Yeah, it's a pretty big wallet.

IT'S JUST AMAZING how much of my free time I spend running errands. And it's amazing how many of those errands involve going to the drugstore. And it's amazing how much I spend at the drugstore even though I was just there a few days ago. Of course, whenever I go to CVS, I proceed to make an ass out of myself. You see, I'm one of those guys who refuse to take a cart or a basket while shopping—oh no, that's too effeminate for me. So instead I awkwardly attempt to carry all my items through the store in a giant bear hug and usually as I reach the end of each aisle, I drop something. Then when I bend to pick it up, I drop something else, and so on. Chicks are zooming by me with carts left and right and I'm trying to figure out how to carry an eight-pack of Charmin with just my pinky and index fingers.

CURRENTLY, I AM in the midst of performing a cruel and unusual experiment on myself. Tired of craving this horribly addictive product, I am attempting to wean myself off ChapStick. It is proving to be much more difficult than I expected. They should call it CrackStick.

I THINK THAT cell phone store employees are like an all-star team of the most incompetent, slow, rude, and lazy people on the planet. But the beauty of the cell phone store is that the employees aren't half as bad as the customers. I've never seen more customers who can't read instructions, don't follow signs, and are generally unable to function in society than at the cell phone store. When you have incompetent salespeople completely ignoring dozens of illiterate customers who are all on the wrong line anyway, you get utter chaos. If your phone breaks, trust me, just throw it out and buy a new one online.

I DO THE vast majority of my shopping online these days. One of the reasons is that I hate going into stores where it's not clear right away which stuff is men's and which is women's. The worst is when you're looking at a shirt and the salesperson causally comes up behind you and tells you it's a woman's sweater. You're always like, "Yeah, um, I knew that, it's for my sister." And then you get the hell out of there.

MEMO TO PEOPLE wearing T-shirts from Urban Outfitters: "thrift store" T-shirts aren't cool if they cost thirty bucks and everyone has the same one.

WHENEVER I GET a spam email with the subject "Stop paying for porn!" I think to myself, who's paying?

I JUST SIGNED up for this service called Upromise so now whenever I use my American Express card, a small sum of money is automatically contributed to my three-year-old cousin Daniel's college fund. I feel good knowing that when I go out binge drinking and wasting my education, I'm actually helping Daniel pay for his education. And maybe one day he can waste it, too. I know it's a dream, but it's my dream.

HOW COME I can never fill out forms properly the first time? You know, you accidentally put the city and state in the "city" box and the ZIP code in the "state" box and then you get to the "ZIP code" box and realize that you're a fucking idiot.

I LOVE WHEN someone at the pizza place tries to pay with a fifty-dollar bill and the cashier holds it up to the light and studies it closely like he's some kind of counterfeiting expert. Stick to slicing pepperoni, chief.

WHY ARE THE taxes on my cell phone bill more than the bill itself?

I FINALLY GOT what I have been saving up for for a while—LASIK eye surgery. Here's the deal. First you go in there and they show you a video about the procedure. It shows a guy being operated on and the next thing you know he's Jet Skiing. I said, "Sign me up!" Then a nurse asked me a few questions such as "Do you drink alcohol never, occasionally, or a lot?" I was like, "Um, how about occasionally I drink a lot?" The procedure itself lasts all of six minutes. They sit you in a chair and tape your eyelids open *Clockwork Orange*–style. When the laser is actually correcting your eye you don't really feel anything, but it sort of smells. My eyeballs happened to smell like mesquite. After the procedure, the same nurse told me to take prescription eye drops at breakfast, lunch, dinner, and before bed. I said, "So 2 P.M., 5 P.M., 9 P.M. and 3 A.M.?" She replied, "Why don't you just do it every four hours. Wiseass." Almost immediately after the surgery I had better than perfect vision. It's truly amazing. The best part was that I charged the whole operation on my credit card and used the points to go Jet Skiing—how's that for poetic justice?

I LOVE WHEN I buy something and it comes to like $5.01. There's always that awkward silence after you pay with a ten-dollar bill when you're waiting for the cashier to tell you to forget about the one cent. You're vainly searching your pockets for change, you're looking for that penny tray next to the register, you do that little under-your-breath snicker, and finally the cashier gives you five bucks back and all is good in the world once again.

HAVE YOU NOTICED that in all the stores now you swipe your own credit or debit card? What genius came up with this idea? Whatever time is supposed to be saved by free-ing up the cashier to do other things is more than lost when I bumble about trying to read the hieroglyphics on the machine that tells me which way to swipe my card.

DO YOU GET nervous when you go to buy something at a store and they actually watch you sign the receipt to see if it matches the signature on your credit card? I'm always like, oh, shit, I forgot exactly how I loop my *K*, I hope she doesn't notice!

I DO ALL my banking online. I rarely write checks, but when I do, I'm faced with the horrifying fact that I have no idea how to write in script anymore. I'm making it up as I go along, a squiggle there, a dot here. And there you have it, folks, I have an Ivy League education but I failed cursive.

I AM VERY confused about the price of underwear. Do you realize that a pair of brand-name underwear is like nine bucks? I don't get it. How do people wear Polo underwear every day? Either they do laundry every three days or they've spent several hundred dollars on underwear. Either one is pretty weird in my book.

EVER GET A solicitation from your alma mater asking for a donation in the same stack of mail as your student loan bill? That's it . . . there's no joke here. I was just wondering if that ever happened to you. I think you can supply the irony yourself on this one.

HOW COME EVERY time I go to book a flight online, I find the flight I want and say, you know what, I'll just book this tomorrow—then I go back the next day and the price has gone up by about $900!?

WHY DOES THE bank close so early? I bet the last time

you rushed to make it to the bank before it closed, you didn't make it. Who can when it closes at 3:30 P.M.? But maybe, just maybe, the bank does it on purpose to save you the shame of realizing how little business you have to transact in the first place. Or, they're just dicks.

WHEN I'M NOT rushing to the bank, much of my free time is spent either eating, thinking of eating, planning on eating, or resting in a state of having just eaten. I can't cook. (The only pizza I've ever made had perforations in it. Even in elementary school when on the holidays every kid baked cupcakes or something, I always volunteered to bring in napkins instead.) So, I take out almost every meal. Sometimes, though, I'll meet a friend for dinner, usually when I'm sick of ordering from establishments where "double meat" is an option.

EVERY NEW YORKER has them. In a drawer, on a table, in the closet. Menus. Hundreds of them, most left by furtive delivery men who jam them under your door. And we all have the same stack: 400 menus, one deli, one pizza place, one Chinese place, and 397 Japanese restaurants, including Yeah Sushi, Yo Sushi, Go Sushi, and Ho Sushi. And they all suck.

EATING OUT CAN get very stressful. For instance, when you're about to order but you're not sure if the other person is going to get something to start with so you don't know if you should either. It's like appetizer Russian roulette. Then there's that awkward moment that occurs when you're in mid-conversation but then that guy with the strange crumb scraper thing comes and methodically removes every morsel from the tablecloth while you and your friend sit in strained silence and try not make eye contact either with each other or the busboy. And you think to yourself, you know, double meat doesn't sound so bad right now.

EVER NOTICE THAT when you're sitting at a restaurant and the waiter comes over to take your order, you instinctively reopen and look at your menu even though you know exactly what you want?

ONE OF MY number-one pet peeves: waiters who make you feel bad about ordering tap water. Waiter: "Would you care for an overpriced bottle of sparkling water?" Me: "Uh, no thanks, regular water is fine." Waiter: "Oh, so just plain tap water? From the sink in the bathroom in the back? Of course, sir, right away, sir, I'll be back in a moment with two dirty glasses."

FOR SOME REASON I always get screwed with the seating arrangements at big dinners. If it's a round table, then everyone has an equal opportunity to make and be part of the conversation. But I always show up late when there's a big, rectangular table and all the good seats at the midpoints of each side are taken, so I end up all the way at one end next to the guy that nobody knows, desperately trying to listen in to figure out why everyone in the middle is laughing and hoping it's not about me.

YOU KNOW WHEN you get seated at a diner and one person is in the booth and the other is in a chair? I think which seat you choose says a lot about your personality. For instance, I always choose the chair. I prefer the ability to adjust my position in any direction because I'm a person who likes to be in control. Also, the booth makes my ass sweat.

SITTING OUTSIDE TO eat is never as good an idea as you think it will be. You're always like, it's such a nice day, let's get a table outside! Next thing you know your napkins are blowing away, the one person sitting in the sun is too hot, you're freezing, there are bugs everywhere, and you're just praying that the big, rectangular table inside is still available.

I DON'T GET it when menus have entrees listed that say they are "homemade." Do they live in the restaurant or something?

EVER LISTEN TO the radio and you hear this great new song and it's two minutes before you realize it's a Sprite commercial?

I HATE PEOPLE who hold up the line by asking for a "taste" of ice cream before deciding what to order. These flavors are not new, they're just combinations of other flavors you've already tried! Besides, you look like an idiot slurping out of that miniature spoon.

I LOVE HOW I look at the Nutrition Facts on a box of food like I have any idea what I'm reading. I'm like, ooh, 50% of my recommended daily intake of Riboflavin? I'll take two!

EVER NOTICE THAT the drink does not increase in proportion to the rest of the value meal when you supersize? You get the same size sandwich, a couple of extra fries, and like a two-gallon drum of Diet Coke. Who can drink that much?

I DON'T KNOW about you, but when I go out to eat, I go to get fed. Just serve me the food ready to eat! I don't want buffets or smorgasbords and I certainly don't want to make-my-own or build-my-own anything! I just want to fucking eat! If I order fajitas, don't serve me chicken on one plate, guacamole and sour cream in another dish, and lettuce and onions in another. Wrap that mother fucker up for me—you're the chef, why the hell would you think I can do it better than you?

ANOTHER THING I hate: garbage cans with a swinging lid at fast food restaurants. Am I the only the one who has a problem with this? Basically, you have two options. You can either attempt to push the lid in using your tray while at the same time making sure your half-eaten burger and two-gallon drum of soda don't spill all over the place, or you can actually touch that swinging lid of filth to keep it open while you drop your garbage in. Either way you're screwed.

YOU KNOW WHAT freaks me out about restaurant bathrooms? The "Employees Must Wash Hands" sign. To me, this implies that restaurant employees need to be reminded to wash their hands before returning to work. I can just imagine the conversation between chefs in the bathroom: "Hey, Jack, did you know you had to wash your hands after taking a shit?" "Really?" "Yeah, it says so right here on this sign."

WHY ARE ALL food delivery men only four feet tall? And why do they insist on riding their bicycles kamikaze style down the wrong side of the street? And have you ever seen a female delivery person?

SOME ESTABLISHMENTS REALLY need to employ a copy editor for their menus. What always bothers me is the misplacement of quotation marks at Chinese restaurants. What does "lunch" special mean? Why is "lunch" in quotes? I can understand if maybe "special" was in quotes, or even "lunch special," but just "lunch"? I mean, if they're misusing punctuation, how good could the dumplings be?

I HAVE A coupon for Domino's pizza. On the bottom, it says "Drivers carry less than $20." Right above it says, "Special: Two Large Pizzas and 2-Liter Soda, $21.99." So what happens when I give the guy $21.99, he can't accept it?

I LOVE WATCHING people dab the top of a slice of pizza with a napkin to try to soak up some of the grease. Oh yeah, now it's just like eating a rice cake.

MEMO TO FOOD service employees: if you leave those latex gloves on all day, including when you handle money and blow your nose, it kind of defeats the purpose.

PRETTY MUCH EVERY night, my roommate Brian and I try to find the culinary Holy Grail of twentysomething life: take-out that is healthy, cheap, and good. It's nearly impossible. Food that is cheap and good is very rarely healthy. And anything both good and healthy is never cheap. Your best bet is to get two out of three and let either your taste buds, your gut, or your wallet take the hit. And from the look of the guts on me and Brian, I'd say healthy lost the battle and the war.

BUT ALL IS not lost due to my horrendous eating habits. After all, I belong to a really fancy gym. I don't know, maybe even a little too fancy. The first time I went in there this guy wearing Spandex took me on a tour of the place. He was all perky like, "Here is the spa, next to it is the aerobics center, and over there is the double-paned, temperature-controlled, soundproof yoga facility!" I was like, dude, can you show me some weights or something, 'cause I'm starting to feel a little uncomfortable.

I'VE FOUND THAT when I'm on the treadmill, I tend to slyly glance at the person next to me to see how fast she's running. Like we're in some sort of crazy race that goes nowhere.

IT SEEMS THAT lately, more and more girls I know have been joining my fancy gym. That in itself I don't mind. I just hate when I bump into one of them and I'm all sweaty and she's all sweaty and there's that awkward moment where I'm not sure if I should give her a kiss on the cheek and we both sort of pause in mid-hug until one of us finally says, "Ugh, I'm disgusting" then we both chuckle, say hello, wipe our brows, and get on with the rest of our lives.

WHO ARE THESE people who drink coffee while working out? These are usually the same people who leave the gym and immediately light up a cigarette. In other words, idiots.

EVER NOTICE THAT no matter how diligent you are about regularly going to the gym, the one day you slack off you end up walking right past it, and it silently taunts you? Conversely, if the only thing you do in an entire day is go to the gym, it's a good day. Because you can say to yourself, well, at least I worked out today.

HAVE YOU EVER gone to the gym and done that half-ass workout? You know, you're tired, you're hungover, but you know if you go to the gym, you'll feel a little bit better, so you just go there and attempt to convince yourself that you already worked out that day? You're like, well, I did lift that box earlier this morning, so that's pecs. And I had to stick my arm out forever to get a cab, so that's triceps. And my gym bag is so heavy, so that's biceps. Great, all I need to do is bend over to pick up that towel, that'll be my abs workout, and I'm outta here!

WHY IS THERE a sign outside the sauna in the men's

locker room of my gym that says "Do not use if pregnant"?

MY FANCY GYM has some pretty wacky aerobics classes. Without fail, there's always that one, solitary dude in every session full of women. Hey, if you feel comfortable taking a cardio-striptease class, then more power to you, man.

ONE OF MY friends kept telling me I should try taking a spinning class at the gym. I'm always like, come on, I'm lifting weights here, spinning is for chicks. The other day I was at the gym and I saw a bunch of pretty cute girls go into the spinning room, so I decided to take the class. Hey, I played high school soccer, how tough could this be? But there, at the front of the room, was the man who would become my arch nemesis—Stefan, the spinning instructor from hell. Wearing a headset microphone, he could only be described as a stationary bike televangelist, barking orders from his pulpit as Acapulco-style trance music blasted from the stereo. With a thick German accent, he yelled things like, "And eight, and five, and three, two, one, out of the saddle, now break away!" and started pedaling furiously. Meanwhile I'm thinking, oh God, help, help me, my quads are exploding, make it stop, why aren't any of these chicks hyperventilating like me!? By the end of the 45-minute session my body had reached the dew point—I was saturated with sweat. But I'll be back, Stefan, oh yes, I'll be back. Maybe.

HOW COME WHEN another guy and I are the only people in the entire gym locker room do our lockers always end up being right next to each other? And why is the guy always so ugly, so hairy, and so naked?

WHY DO PEOPLE in the locker room, when they get out of the shower, do that little barefoot walk on the sides of their feet? Is that supposed to prevent athlete's foot or something? Like the germs are going, "Oh, wait, this guy is only walking on the sides of his feet, we can't touch that. Let's hold out for some heel."

I'VE NOTICED THAT, when working out, people always wear clothes from the last organized league they played in. The huge guy doing squats has his college lacrosse shorts on, I'm there with a shirt from my high school soccer team, and the fat dude in the corner wearing his junior high tennis shirt and a headband, well, you know he hasn't been to the gym in a while.

GUYS DON'T DO yoga. Guys do, however, enjoy watching women in spandex thongs stretch suggestively. Thus, merely watching yoga is OK.

THE GYM IS full of people pretending not to look in the mirror. Guys are taking a drink from the water fountain, sneaking a peak at their abs, picking up a towel, checking out their biceps. Everyone is pretending not to look. I say we screw all this pretend nonsense. We're all in the gym so that we look better in the mirror, so why is looking in the mirror at the gym such a bad thing? Hell, I'm full-out flexing and I'm the smallest dude there.

HOW COME I can run three miles on the treadmill with no problem, but if later in the day I run up three flights of stairs I think I'm gonna have a heart attack?

SOMETIMES I'LL WATCH TV while running on the treadmill and see a commercial for a gym where there are tons of hot chicks running the treadmill, and I'll look around at all the ugly people running the treadmill next to me and think, am I in the wrong gym?

I LOVE WATCHING these guys in the gym who feel the

need to attach unnecessary amounts of weight to themselves while doing normal exercises. Like the guy who wears wrist weights, ankle weights, and a belt around his waist with a forty-five-pound plate hanging from it just to do chin-ups. Then he can only do like two reps and he gets all pissed off. Dude, lighten up. Literally.

RECENTLY, HOWEVER, MY fancy gym raised its rates on me astronomically. Apparently, in order to continue to qualify for a "corporate discount," it's necessary to actually "be employed." Either way, I could no longer afford the new rate. I pleaded with them, but they wouldn't budge a penny. I was forced to cancel my membership. I couldn't believe that after three years, my gym was letting me go just like that, without a fight. Didn't our relationship mean anything? Was I just another pretty face on a laminated identification card? A few days later, though, they did let me come back and collect the belongings that I had left in the locker room over the years. As I walked out, I took a final look at the cast of characters I had been working out alongside every morning—Stefan the evil spinning instructor, the hot MILF, the unusually jacked old guy, the foreign model, the grunter, the sweater, the bench-press reps bettor. I didn't know what the future held as I passed through the exit turnstile one last time. I was frightened and alone. Scared, even. Then on my way home I passed a gym that wasn't too expensive and was a lot closer to my apartment, so actually it worked out pretty well in the end.

A DAY IN the life of a twentysomething generally takes us from the bank to the deli to the gym and then back to the bank again. But despite my erratic spending, eating, and exercising habits, I still get along pretty well for myself in all three categories. I've managed not to feel too fat, broke, or hungry, at least not all at the same time. There's only one thing I'm pissed about, though: I'm all but disqualified from playing on *The Price Is Right*. Seriously, I was watching the show the other day while running the treadmill at my new, not so fancy gym, and I was so far off on all the prices because everything is so expensive in Manhattan and I never cook. I'm thinking a bottle of dishwasher detergent is like 15 bucks and the answer is $3.99. If I was on the show, I'd have to be that annoying guy who bets one dollar every time, hopes everyone else busts, and wins by default. Still, I lament, with all the trips I make to the ATM and drugstore, I will probably never make it to the Showcase Showdown. Fuck me.

EIGHT

the big city

I moved to Manhattan following graduation and, if I could, would never live anywhere else. I grew up on Long Island and therefore the city has always been close to me both in spirit and proximity, but you never get to know the true meaning of Gotham until you've lived here for a while. While the rent is high, the apartments tiny, the summers sweltering, the cabbies rude, the streets dirty, and the subway confusing, New York is somehow still the best damn town in the world. How is this contradiction possible? Well, let's examine twentysomething life in the big city.

For one, New York is so amazing because it's so unique. Where else can you hit on preppy Columbia chicks on the Upper West Side and hippie NYU chicks in the East Village . . . in the same night? Where else can an intersection have a red light glowing in all four directions simultaneously . . . and cars and people are still screaming through? Where else do guys on the corner magically appear selling umbrellas . . . when it only started raining 90 seconds ago? And where else can you pay thousands of dollars in rent for an apartment with a sofa bed . . . but not have enough room to actually unfold the bed?

I get a lot of emails from people who lived in the city for the first time as a summer intern. They tell me about what an amazing time they had and about all the museums and attractions and incredible restaurants they went to. And I think to myself, how come I live here year-round and never do any of that? New York City, though, is not for everyone. It's fast-paced and expensive and the incense they sell in the street really stinks. But if you're single and twentysomething, I can't imagine where else you'd rather be. So to summer interns, NYU freshmen, and umbrella salesmen alike, I say, "Welcome. Life, in the big city, is good."

I LOVE HOW people not from New York can't comprehend how loud it is here. Whenever my agent calls me from Los Angeles and I'm on Third Avenue with sirens blaring everywhere, he's always like, "Karo, man, are you *in* the ambulance?"

I BELONG TO a New York subculture that I have coined the "Big Ten." The Big Ten consists of everyone in Manhattan between the ages of twenty-two and twenty-five who went to Michigan, Wisconsin, Indiana, Penn, Cornell, Florida, Maryland, Emory, Binghamton, or Syracuse. Whenever you go to a bar in Big Ten territory (roughly Fifteenth to Fiftieth on the East Side), each member of the Big Ten must send a representative. It's sort of like the Olympics. We even have our own uniforms. For guys, it's Diesel jeans with the classic blue button-down shirt untucked with the sleeves rolled up slightly. For girls, it's those pointy-toed elf shoes, a little shoulder bag tucked snugly under the left arm, and, if it's raining, one of those stupid caps with the small brim. We even have our own holiday, Thanksgiving Eve, which is when future Big Tenners come home from college and flock to the city for the second most inebriated night of the year behind New Year's.

AN IMPORTANT TERM to learn if you live in New York is "B&T." B&T, short for "bridge and tunnel," is a derogatory term used by people in Manhattan to describe people from New Jersey, Brooklyn, Queens, and Long Island who come to Manhattan (via bridge or tunnel) to party on the weekends. Used in a sentence, someone in the Big Ten might say, "Oh, God, this bar is sooo B&T." You might wonder how we can tell if someone is a B&Ter or not. You'll just have to trust me, we can. The Big Ten vs. the B&T crowd is a vicious rivalry. However, being that I am originally from Long Island, I am a former B&Ter myself, so I tend to cut these guys some slack.

EVERY TIME I meet someone from New Jersey, I ask them what town they are from. And every time they tell me I just stare at them blankly. Why? Because I don't know any fucking towns in New Jersey!

I GREW UP in Plainview, a town on Long Island about forty minutes east of the city. What's good about having my parents live so close by is that I'm able to come home for all the major holidays—Thanksgiving, Mother's Day, Father's Day, you know, the usual. What's bad is that every time I come home, I'm so fucking hungover that I end up spending the entire day sleeping on the couch in the living room.

BACK IN COLLEGE, you used to worry about "hallcest," or hooking up with someone on the same floor as you in your dorm and then running into them awkwardly all the time. In the city it's even worse. We have "buildingcest," whereby if you hook up with someone who lives in the same apartment building, you run the risk of uncomfortable elevator rides for the rest of your lease. And it gets worse. We're so on top of each other here that I've even experienced "windowcest." This girl I hooked up with lives in the building across the street and we can see in each other's bedrooms. Now I have to walk around with the blinds closed all the time.

I'M ACTUALLY LIVING in my second apartment since I came to New York. Moving within the city is a fate I would not wish upon my worst enemy. I only moved four blocks up Third Avenue. My roommate and I calculated that we moved about a thousand feet door to door. Where else in the world can you move a thousand feet, have it cost you a thousand dollars, and still be able to see into the bedroom of the last girl you hooked up with?

EVERYTHING THAT I had in my room at school that I thought had a few more years left in it I took with me to New York. The rest of my apartment is furnished by a well-known foreign designer. His name is IKEA. I bought a funky, comfortable chair at IKEA. I thought it was different. I have so far seen the same chair in at least six different twentysomething's apartments. I didn't realize it came in so many colors. This IKEA guy must be making a fortune.

MAKE ANY COMMENT about a person's apartment, good or bad, and you'll always be met with the same response: "Oh, I'm never home anyway." Really? Well, I guess you don't have to worry about windowcest then.

NEW YORK CITY apartments are pretty tight. In my bathroom, I have to keep all of my toiletries on a shelf above the toilet. This gets interesting. About once a week I have to go diving across the room to swat away my floss as it's about to fall off into the toilet. One time my electric toothbrush fell off the shelf and my hands were full so I flung my foot out, nipped the brush with my toe, and it hit the side of the bowl and landed safely on the bathmat. It was one of the greatest bathroom moments of my life.

HAVE YOU EVER noticed that if you are up late in a really quiet house or apartment, the sounds coming from the door down the hall always sound like people having sex? It could be the TV or the stereo or just someone talking on the phone, but for a brief second, your sexual radar pops up. And of course you creep up to the door to get a better listen, but you're always disappointed when it's a false alarm.

WHEN DID EVERYONE become so obsessed with candles? I can't walk into an apartment anymore without being besieged by twenty different burning aromas. And I love the people who have candles but never use them. There's always that lighter sitting neatly in the wax tray, just begging to be used, but you can't be the first otherwise everyone will know it was you who stunk up the bathroom.

THERE'S JUST SOMETHING about bar soap that I find disgusting. You know when you're in a bathroom and you're washing up and instead of liquid soap you spot the dish? You know, the dish with the slimy bar soap just marinating there in the last person's grime? I don't trust any kind of soap that you actually need to clean off before you use.

YOU KNOW WHAT also freaks me out? Wet finger-prints on the toilet paper roll. It's bad enough that you're in someone else's bathroom, have to use bar soap, and have no idea which hand towel to use without having to look at the phantom presence of the previous shitter!

THE OTHER DAY, I had to pick up a piece of nice fake art for my apartment. In case you didn't know, it is required for former frat boys living in New York to have Picasso prints hanging in our common rooms. It makes us look distinguished.

WHEN I HAVE dinner at my place, I sit hunched over on a sofa bed in the halogen bulb-lit common room of my tiny apartment eating take-out off an IKEA coffee table while sipping grocery store brand cola out of gas station souvenir glasses adorned with football helmets from teams that have since relocated. I'm not even sure that qualifies as human.

MY APARTMENT HAS a doorman. Surprisingly, this does not give me the peace of mind I thought it would. For one, my doorman assumes anyone entering the building who looks under the age of thirty is there to see me and lets them upstairs—then calls me when they are already coming up in the elevator. Presumably this includes baby-faced burglars and serial killers. I'm also running out of things to say to the doorman when I come and go every day. "How are you?" "Take it easy." "Catch you later." "Have a good one." It's embarrassing to admit, but the other day I actually said, "How's it hanging?"

I DREAD THE moment when I get in the elevator of my building and press my floor but then another guy jumps into the elevator at the last moment and goes to press his floor, only to realize that it's already pressed. Am I obligated to introduce myself to him because he lives on my floor? Do we really need to make idle conversation about the state of the building's air conditioning system? Must I say "hey" accompanied by a subtle head nod every time I see him in the lobby thereafter? Sometimes I wish I lived in a walk-up.

HOW COME I am completely unable to operate the doors of other people's apartments? You know, when you go to leave and you turn the knob that you're not supposed to touch and then turn the other knob the wrong way and then you lock yourself in even more and you can't remember which way you turned what and you end up yanking helplessly at the door until your friend mercifully comes to your rescue and lets you out.

WHY DO CAB drivers get so upset when you hit traffic? It's not like they're getting out.

HOW COME EVERY deli in New York has at least one word spelled wrong in the window?

WHY IS IT that whatever someone else is reading on the subway is always so interesting?

DOESN'T IT SEEM like there's more scaffolding than sky in New York these days?

HOW COME EVERY time I walk down the street and get hit with water dripping from an air conditioner it still confuses the hell out of me?

NEW YORK IS full of people. Here are some that irk, annoy, or otherwise piss me off. People who call you to ask for a phone number, but then don't have a pen ready when you give it to them. People who brag about how few books they've read. People who prefer Raisinets over Goobers. People who act like they're having an epileptic seizure when they win a radio contest. People who try to bum cigarettes off me even though I don't smoke. Smokers who complain about other smokers bumming cigarettes off them. People who leave their cell phone on when they take naps then act surprised when I call and wake them up. People who hide the kitchen garbage can in the cabinet below the sink. People who say their favorite basketball player is Michael Jordan. People who insist on playing pool in really crowded bars. People who try to pound your fist instead of give you a handshake. People who shave their sideburns two inches *above* their ear line. People who clap at airplane landings. People who slow down when they see a cop on the side of the road giving someone *else* a ticket. People who hold their breath manually when they jump into the pool. People who carry both cell phones and beepers. People who bring cheap beer to parties then drink the expensive stuff that other people brought. Dry cleaners who tell you that your clothes will be ready in a week but if you ask them if they can have it ready by tomorrow they can. Anyone wearing a wristband while not exercising. College graduates who still have their mom schedule their dentist appointments. Thirty-year-old chicks with belly button rings. Guys wearing polo shirts with the collar turned up. Girls wearing those furry winter boots . . . in the summer. And, finally, anyone wearing a chain that connects their wallet to their jeans, which wasn't even cool when it *was* cool—in 1996.

TO ME, SUMMER in New York City is like going through puberty. Beforehand, you're both apprehensive and excited about what lies ahead. Then, you don't even realize it's under way until halfway through when you start breaking out and can't stop thinking about girls. And when it's all over, your memory of what actually happened is fuzzy, the frequent awkward moments replaced forever in your mind with sporadic instances of glory.

ONE OF THE benefits of living in the financial and media capital of the world is that New York is also the summer intern capital of the world. The NYU dorms in Union Square are emptied of their usual nose-ring-clad residents and instead filled with hard-partying investment banking summer analysts. The outdoor bars will be packed from happy hour to closing. And the girls, well, the girls, the girls . . . wait, is it me . . . or did all the girls just get really hot all of a sudden?

YES, WITH ALL the interns in the city during the summer, the skirts are short, the IDs are fake, the IQs are low, but the chicks are hot! I remember I was at a bar talking to this really cute girl. We were definitely hitting it off. I bought her a few drinks but she seemed kind of nervous that the bartender would card her. I told her to relax because there are always underage college chicks there and no one cares. She said, "But I'm only a junior." "So what?" I said. "In high school." Um, check please!

WE ALL TRY to do it, but let's be honest, it's really awkward trying to walk in flip-flops. I know it's the summer and we're trying to be all casual, but it's just not working. Our feet are dirty, our calves ache, that space between the big toe and the toe next to it is all cut up, and we look like fools when one sandal flies off and we're forced to do the one-legged hop to retrieve it. Let's face it, it's time to give up.

I LOVE THE annual July 4th fireworks show in New York, but is it really necessary to say, "Hey, look at that one!" every time a particularly bright one goes off? The fireworks are exploding in the middle of the clear sky above the East River and we're standing on the roof of a thirty-story apartment building. Dude, I can see them all.

UNFORTUNATELY, THE SUMMER is also when New York is besieged by tourists. I fucking hate tourists. Actually, let me qualify that statement. I only hate tourists because some New Yorkers are so dumb that they can't tell the difference between tourists and regular people. I'll be walking in midtown, minding my own business, when a red-vested asshole will tap me on the shoulder and ask, "Excuse me, sir, would you like a double-decker bus tour of the city?" Hmm . . . let me think about that . . . do I motherfucking look like I want a double-decker tour of the city? Do you see a digital camera on me? Am I wearing a yellow Yankees cap or unusually high tube socks? Why don't you try asking the twenty people from Kansas behind you who are actually taking pictures of the *bus?*

AND JUST IN case you're new to the city and can't spot the tourists, they usually come in groups of four: the father is slightly overweight and sports a mustache, the mother is holding a map and wearing a visor, the son is holding on to his mom's leg and whining, and the daughter, walking five feet ahead of the rest of her family, is dressed unusually slutty for someone her age.

ONE OF THE most reviled enemies in *Ruminations on College Life* were the notorious "slow walkers," those bastards who stroll leisurely side by side in front of you, preventing you from getting by when you're late for class. I hate to say this, but since I graduated and moved to New York, the problem has only gotten worse. The sidewalks are filled to the curb with fucking idiots who can't seem to get it through their thick heads that people behind them are trying to get by. So slow walkers, listen up! Here are the rules: First, never walk parallel with more than two people! If you're in a big group, form a column. Second, don't stop suddenly and look up! If there is a monument or other assorted building you would like to gaze at longingly, pull over to the side before you do so. Third, if a blinking street sign says "Don't Walk," that means *GO!* The only reason you should be waiting on the corner is if you're a police cadet or seeing-eye dog. And finally, for the love of God, if you want to take a picture with your slow-walker family, don't choose the most congested walkway possible in the middle of lunch hour in the pouring rain and stop all pedestrian traffic both ways while you fiddle with your fucking camera phone and solicit uninterested passersby who can't operate a flash to snap a blurry photo. This is New York City, you will be killed. Thank you, this has been a public service announcement from the pissed off guy behind you.

EVERY SUMMER, COLLEGE grads flock to the Big Apple to try to find the perfect apartment. And that means dealing with one of the country's most notorious swindlers: the New York City apartment broker. Never have such a collection of poorly trained charlatans controlled such important assets. Here's a typical conversation between a newly minted college grad from the Midwest and her rapidly balding broker: "I've got an amazing apartment for you, you'll love it." "Really? In the East Village?" "No, it's a little farther uptown, uh, Upper West Side actually. But it's beautiful, I promise." "Um, OK, it's a three-bedroom though, right?" "It's actually a studio . . . but it's huge! You'll love it, I promise." "Uh, OK, how much is it?" "It's a little out of your price range but we can always knock it down. Why don't you just come see it? It's unbelievable. I'm telling you, it's got like five exposures, beautiful hardwood floors, it's beautiful." "Sounds great, have *you* seen it?" "Well . . . actually, no."

NEW YORK IS all about location. Some people have not figured this out yet. It cracks me up when a friend moves into an awesome new apartment in an out-of-the-way part of the city. There's just no point. My buddy Eric once told me, "Yo, Karo, I just got this huge two-bedroom in the financial district, you have to come over to pre-game one night." I just said flat-out, "Listen, man, that's great, but I guarantee you that between now and when you move out, I will not see your apartment once."

OK, I WILL spot Los Angeles one, *one* advantage over New York. Better weather. This is pretty much how the summer has played out in New York for the past few years: It starts with a period of six weeks where it rains every single day. Then we have about a month where it's nice during the week until Thursday at 5 P.M. when a vicious monsoon descends upon the city and doesn't abate until Sunday morning, thereby ruining the entire weekend. That is usually followed by two straight weeks of 95 degree balls-stuck-to-the-inside-of-your-thigh heat with the occasional air conditioner–canceling city-wide blackout thrown in for good measure. Let me try to put this all in perspective for you. The weather in New York is so bad sometimes, it has actually become fashionable to talk about it. No longer is the weather relegated to first-date icebreakers and elevator small talk. People are actually interested in the weather. Weather is in! Weather is the new black!

WILL SOMEONE PLEASE tell me why they still make umbrellas with pointy spokes on them? You would think it's common sense that anything wielded at eye-level with limited visibility should be rounded at the ends.

WHO ARE THESE people at Starbucks who sit all day staring out the window and scribbling in little note-books?

I NEVER REALIZED how many people lived in Manhattan until I got the Yellow Pages. The thing's so big we use it as extra seating when guests come over.

THE MOST NOTORIOUS cell phone talkers I have ever seen are New York City cab drivers. These guys are on their cell phones literally all day. They'll be talking away your entire ride. Why do they have more friends than me? And what could they possibly be talking about? They're definitely not discussing the fastest and cheapest way to get to your destination, I can tell you that much.

WHEN YOU'RE WAITING for a cab for what seems like forever and every one that goes by is taken, don't you start looking at the cabs like they're limos? A cab goes by with someone in the back and you're like, "Wow, how did he swing that? He must be somebody!"

IT STILL BOGGLES my mind that there are people out there without cell phones. How do they live? How do they make plans or meet anyone? Remember the last time you met someone somewhere in the city? How many phone calls did it take? Like a dozen, right? "Are you taking a cab?" "Are you close?" "What corner are you on?" "East or West side of the street?" "I can't find you." "Which store?" "OK, I see you, I'm crossing the street." "No, the other street." "I'm directly behind you." "My hand is on your shoulder . . . right . . . now!"

WHAT ABOUT THE obligatory cell phone number exchange? You meet someone you haven't seen for a while in the street and they ask you for your cell phone number. So of course you have to ask them for their cell phone number too, even though you have no intention of calling. Sometimes when I'm pretending to enter in their number, I'm actually just playing Snake.

ANOTHER AWKWARD SITUATION occurs in New York when you are walking down a relatively empty sidewalk and there happens to be a person walking right next to you in the same direction as you at the exact same pace. I never know whether to pass or draft.

WHEN YOU'RE WALKING down the street and you see someone up ahead giving out flyers, you think how annoying those people are. Like I need another flyer for a barber shop or a strip club. But when you walk past the person and they don't try to give you a flyer, don't you get kind of insulted? What, I'm not good enough for your strip club?

OR WHAT ABOUT when you are walking down the street and the only other person on the sidewalk is walking toward you. I never know whether to look at them or pretend not to look at them or really not look at them but inevitably at about ten feet you both look up, make eye contact, quickly avert your eyes, speed up, and pass each other. I really shouldn't leave my apartment anymore.

I WAS A proud member of the Zeta Beta Tau fraternity at Penn. And now that I live in New York, I happen to run into ZBT brothers from other colleges quite frequently. But I have a small request for my fellow alumni. Please stop giving me the secret handshake. Seriously. Because when I shake your hand and feel you start to wiggle your fingers around down there, I always get a little nervous before I figure out what the hell is going on. How about you just come out and tell me we're brothers so that we can avoid any potential misunderstandings? Thank you.

NEW YORK CITY firefighters have long been recognized for their courage. But you know why I really admire firefighters? They handle traffic really well. I've seen a fire truck with its sirens blaring and its lights flashing like crazy trying to fight its way through Times Square rush hour traffic with no one getting out of their way. But if you look at the firemen in the truck, they're always so calm and collected, even though they are battling some of the worst drivers in the world just to get to a burning building and risk their lives. Now that's impressive. I get stuck behind a couple of slow walkers on the sidewalk and I almost have a coronary.

EVER NOTICE THAT guys like to know the "source" of traffic? It's not enough to be stuck in traffic, we need to figure out its origins. "Wow, this is definitely Giants Stadium traffic." "No, dude, it's rush hour." "I think it's holiday shopping traffic." "Must be an accident." "Should we listen to the traffic report on the radio?" "Nah, it's more fun to argue about it."

SOMETIMES DON'T YOU just want to open your car door in the middle of traffic and clothesline that dude on the motorcycle driving between the lanes?

AS THEY SAY, New York is not just a state, but a state of mind. Especially when it comes to driving, New Yorkers think they are God's greatest gift. For example, a few months ago I was driving up north with a buddy and I got stuck behind some jerk who was only doing 80 mph. To no one in particular I yelled out, "Hey, asshole, go back to Vermont!" To which my friend leaned over and said, "Karo, we're in Vermont."

I FEEL BAD for people who are not from a well-known place or who moved around a lot as a kid. Because when you ask them where they're from, they either pick the nearest big city but tell you the exact distance from that city to their hometown, or launch into a whole explanation of all the places they moved to and why. Seriously, just say Phoenix or something, because I really could care less.

EVER REALIZE THAT when the light turns red and you are still in the middle of the street and you do that little hybrid jog/skip/walk where you flail your arms about like an idiot you are actually moving at the same speed as if you just plain walked instead?

THE OTHER DAY, I passed a hot girl with a dog outside of Gramercy Park so I stopped to pet it. I have never in my life guessed the correct sex of a dog. If I say, "Oh, he's really friendly," the owner will say with a scowl,

"Actually it's a she." If later I spot a dog and say, "Oh, she's really cute," the owner will hiss, "Actually it's a he." Oh yeah, well, if you're so smart, why are you picking up shit off the street?

IN THE END, life in Manhattan isn't as daunting as some make it out to be. As it turns out, the big city is actually a pretty small world. For instance, my sister, Caryn, was visiting me once and we were walking down the street together. When we got to a corner, my cell phone rang and a person I really didn't want to talk to popped up on caller ID. I immediately hit the "decline" button on my phone and sent it straight to voice mail. I started telling my sister this funny story about the guy who called and I was making all kinds of faces and gestures and generally making fun of the kid. A few blocks later, I checked my voice mail. The message: "Karo, I called you because I was standing behind you on the street. Asshole." Fuck me.

NINE

twenty-five

The countdown to that most dreaded of milestones, my twenty-fifth birthday, actually began in earnest over a year earlier, on Valentine's Day 2003. On that day, a date that will live in infamy, my friend Danielle became the first twentysomething I knew to get engaged. From that moment on, all signs pointed to the quick and painful end to my early twenties. Danielle's engagement party was followed by a notice of an upcoming high school reunion. My little sister started applying to grad school. My friends started graduating from grad school. My status as a single bachelor came under fire. Danielle got married. My birthday loomed. All hell broke loose.

The irony about the whole situation is that I used to be so mature for my age. I was a precocious little kid.

I picked things up quickly in high school. I had a good head on my shoulders in college. Now, as my early twenties give way to my late twenties, I've all of a sudden become *immature* for my age. Hell, my "terrible twos" just ended last week!

Looking ahead, being twenty-five does have its advantages—I'll actually be able to legally rent a car in most states, and its disadvantages—box wine will probably no longer be considered a suitable gift for most social gatherings. I'd be lying if I said that turning twenty-five didn't scare the hell out of me. But I'd also be lying if I said it wasn't a hell of a ride to get to this point.

Soon, I will have been alive a full quarter-century. This is a time when you must take stock of your life. It is a time to decide whether seriously pursuing a career or continuing to pursue your serious drinking habit is appropriate behavior for someone of your advanced age. In essence, twenty-five is the time to choose between growing up and throwing up. This won't be easy.

I DON'T KNOW what scares me more, the fact that my mom asked me if I want luggage for my twenty-fifth birthday, or the fact that I think I do.

EVER SEE A celebrity on TV, like a new actor or pop singer, who looks about your age, and then you later find out they're like six years younger than you? And it's depressing because even though you can't remember exactly what you were doing at their age, you're pretty sure it wasn't partying at the MTV Beach House or getting laid on a daily basis.

IN HONOR OF my birthday, I decided to write down all of the major things that I accomplished in the last decade of my life. I only wanted to list the most memorable and life-altering events. Here's what I came up with: witnessed Rangers win Stanley Cup, graduated from high school, lost virginity, graduated from college, perfected left-handed masturbation, published book. That's it. Ten years of living and all I have to show for it is two diplomas, a poster, a paperback, a sore wrist, and a lifetime of frustration. Why do I even bother?

ONE THING I think a lot of guys experience as they approach their late twenties is the sudden realization that, like it or not, we're turning into our dads. First, I started getting a bit of a beer belly. Then, I started making that subtle sigh accompanied by a head shake that my dad makes when annoyed. And the other day I found myself saying to a friend that signature dad-phrase, "Don't worry about anyone but yourself." Next thing you know I'll be wearing khaki shorts from Eddie Bauer and a knee brace while sitting on a leather recliner watching the Food Network and munching on pistachio nuts.

YOU KNOW WHAT I'm tired of? People saying, "I'm very disappointed in you." When I was a kid and got in trouble, my parents always gave me that same speech: "We're very disappointed in you." In college, when my fraternity got in trouble, we were told by an administrator, "I'm very disappointed in you." At work, when I messed up, they said, "We're not your parents and this isn't college anymore . . . but we're very disappointed in you." You know what? Shut the fuck up already. I'm about to turn twenty-five and I'm sick of everyone having such high expectations. And when do I get to be the one disappointed, huh?

THE ONLY THING worse than being told "I'm very disappointed in you" is being told that you have to "pay your dues." That's old people's response to everything, isn't it? "Well, you have to pay your dues." "You have to pay your dues first." "Don't worry, you're just paying your dues." Well, how about this? I'm not paying any more dues! Yeah, that's right, I said it. I'm all paid up. No more dues for me. Ha ha ha!! Boy, that felt good.

FOR SOME REASON, I think it's really cool that I was born in 1979. I meet anyone born after me and I'm like, "Dude, you're so eighties. I was born in the seventies, man, yeah!" Right. For the six months I was alive in the seventies, my life consisted of spitting up on myself and babbling incoherently. And if you see me at my birthday party, you'll see that not much has changed.

ONE THING THAT I've always wanted to do was start my own slang. And since this is my book, what the hell. So here's what I've come up with—using the word "gourmet" to mean "cool" or "dope." For instance, one could say "Damn, those sneakers are *gourmet!*" or "That chick you took home last night, man, she was *gourmet!*" I think it's just as good as half the shit rappers come up with. So how about we all start using it and see what happens?

IN MY LAST book, I wrote that college is all about meeting your best friends but at the same time realizing that you'd never trust anyone pre-med or pre-law after seeing them vomit on themselves for four years. Now that we're turning twenty-five, the "pre" is being dropped and some of my buddies are actually becoming doctors and lawyers. That kind of freaks me out. We used to go on drunken rampages—I'd never trust them to operate or litigate! Unless I got a discount, then I'd consider it.

ACCORDING TO SOME of my law school friends, however, you don't have to do any work at all in law school after your first year. Really? Then how come every time I call your cell phone, you pick up whispering in the library? Still, my law school friends who have graduated now finally have real, hard-core jobs for the first time in their lives. Well, it's been fun chilling with you guys for a while, see you in ten years! Suckers.

MED SCHOOL, ACCORDING to what I hear my from my friends, is the opposite of law school. It just keeps getting harder and harder until you go crazy or become a doctor, whichever comes first. Now that's comforting. All I hear from my med school friends these days is complaining about how early they have to get up for their rotations and how tedious their lives have become. I don't understand this. You knew this was going to happen all along. You took bio in college. You studied for the MCATs. You've been in med school for three years. They gave you a stethoscope, for God's sake, what did you think was going to happen?

WITH ALL THIS unexpected stress in their lives, some of my med school friends recently decided to do something very un-late-twenties-like: they went on Spring Break. Little did they know that not everyone would be so receptive to their pale presence on the beaches of Acapulco. My friend Triplet #3 (soon to be Dr. Triplet #3) was making small talk with a girl at a club. He asked her where she went to school. She told him and then asked where he went to school. He told her he already graduated and was now in medical school. She said, "Get a life" and walked away. Oooh, I think the proper medical term for that is "low blow."

IN TRIPLET #3'S defense, though, twenty-five is the age when a guy can pretty much hook up with women of any age, from barely legal to middle-aged. We're just slimy enough to go for the college chicks while just adept enough to bag horny divorcées. Of course, it all gets interesting at the bar when the girl you're with gets carded and she could either be rejected, insulted, flattered, or old enough to be the bouncer's mother.

AT TWENTY-FIVE, MANY people my age still have no idea what they're doing with their lives, so they turn to the age-old fallback: grad school. Now people taking standardized tests in preparation for applying to grad school disturb me for two reasons. One, I am then forced to ask the question, "How was your test?" which is the second most annoying question behind "How was your trip?" And two, I have again begun hearing people say they are "bad test-takers." Mind you these are not people who are dyslexic or have other learning disabilities, it's just that when it comes to test-taking, they are "bad." This has got to be the sorriest excuse in the world. How are you going to be a lawyer or an MBA if you can't pencil in bubbles within an allotted time period?

MY SISTER, CARYN, is moving on up as well, having graduated from Dartmouth and gotten into grad school at UCLA (she's an excellent test-taker, thank you very much). She was telling me how this "woman" in the career services office at Dartmouth was helping her with her grad school applications. I said, "Oh, that's cool, how old is this woman?" And Caryn said, "About your age." I said, "But you called her a 'woman.' Does that make me a man?" "No," my sister replied, "you're still an idiot." It's nice to know some things never change.

ABOUT FOUR MONTHS before my twenty-fifth birthday, I began hooking up with a new girl. She was the high school friend of a buddy of mine from my Wall Street days. Right around the same time, I began to have constant, terrible heartburn but I couldn't figure out what was wrong. It was my roommate, Brian, who finally put two and two together. "Karo," he said, "I don't know how to say this to you, man, but I think you actually like this girl." Shit, I knew I never should have worked on Wall Street!

IT ALSO TURNED out that this girl was a Serial Monogamist, you know, the type who go from boyfriend to boyfriend without ever really dating in between? But she had broken up with her boyfriend the day I met her. This was probably a once-in-a-lifetime opportunity—meeting a Serial Monogamist in the window between boyfriends! I considered calling *National Geographic.*

I THINK THE heartburn began when this girl and I had our first sober hang-out. The first sober hang-out is always, well, a sobering experience. Usually it comes after about three to five late-night drunken booty calls. One of the two parties (usually the girl) suggests hanging out during the day or, even worse, at night but in a non-alcohol-related activity. Even weirder than the first sober hang-out is the first sober hook-up. I mean, before this girl, I don't think I'd hooked up sober in years. It was like I didn't know her ass from her elbow. Literally.

AS I'VE SAID, I spent almost the entirety of my early twenties, including four consecutive years, as a swinging bachelor. But when I met this girl, something changed for me. I think that telling people about a new relationship is like finding out you're pregnant—you don't want to say anything for the first month or two just in case something terrible happens. Hopefully, I'm out of the woods. Yes, that's right, while it may come as a shock to many, soon after meeting this girl, she became my girl-friend. The Serial Monogamist strikes again. How did it happen? Well, we were united by a mutual love of *Family Guy,* drink specials, anything made with four cheeses, and bad weather (since we both work from home and enjoy the suffering of others).

GIRLFRIEND IS A strong woman, I'll tell you that much. She has to be. After all, I have one pair of jeans that I wear every day and rarely wash. I regularly watch the same exact episode of *SportsCenter* twice in a row. I have unusually large calf muscles. I refuse to dance. I have no sense of direction. I have terrible posture. I'm a bathroom-flooder, fast-walker, pen-chewer, and nail-biter. I hate white chocolate, shaving, and karaoke bars. I love black olives, air conditioning, and swim-up bars. One of my armpits is hairier than the other. I need all the bills in my wallet arranged facing the same way and in denomination order at all times. I'm an insomniac—NyQuil actually keeps me up. I can't whistle or tie a scarf. I only drink orange juice with "lots of pulp." I turn my lock to zero before I leave the gym locker room like that is going to foil would-be thieves. I love sushi so much that every time I go out for sushi I order way too much, eat it all, and then get a stomachache. I'm not really a morning person or a night person. I have trouble pronouncing the word "continuity." When I move, I label almost every box "misc.," thereby defeating the purpose of labeling at all. When I tell stories at bars, I tend to gesticulate wildly and knock over nearby beers. My hair is turning red instead of gray. I regularly settle important disputes with rock, paper, scissors (best two of three). I just found out that my whole life I've been snapping incorrectly (I use my thumb and pointer finger). I can't pack a suitcase when people are watching. I go for the first parking spot I see no matter how far away it is. I have to change into a darker shirt before eating anything with red sauce because I always get it all over myself. Yet, I'm so neat, I don't even like when the recycle bin on my computer is full. I have to wash my hands after touching animals, subway poles, money, bathrooms, fast food, strippers, small children, or public mailboxes. Sometimes when someone is running to catch an elevator, I'll pretend to hit "door open" but actually hit "door close." And, finally, I'm fond of writing books where I discuss and make fun of all the intimate details of everyone I've ever met. Oh yeah, this'll last.

THE ARENA WHERE Girlfriend enlightened me first was in the bedroom. Unfortunately, it's not what you think. It began after another rough night of sleep when she told me that I needed sheets with a higher thread count. My response was, "What's a thread count?" Apparently, the spartan decor of my bedroom was adequate for a bachelor, but not a boyfriend. After all, I only have two pillows, a sheet, and a blanket. Girlfriend, on the other hand, has a dust ruffle, a mattress pad, a regular sheet, a top sheet, a fitted sheet, a flat sheet, four blankets, and sixteen pillows. Hell, when she goes into Bed, Bath & Beyond, they greet her by name.

SOMETIMES, IF I'M at a bar and some dude starts hitting on Girlfriend, I'll let him. After all, for the past few years, that guy was me, so I empathize. Only if she's ever really in trouble will I step in and say, "Hey, listen buddy, that's my girlfriend you're hitting on." Hopefully, the next time I do that, the guy will be like, "Really? Damn, she's gourmet."

NOT TO GET ahead of myself or anything, but if I ever get married, there is absolutely no way I'm going to get a joint email address with my wife. Have you seen this?

I get emails from like janeandbobbywilson@aol.com. Oh, that is so very, very lame.

SPEAKING OF MARRIAGE, about a month before my twenty-fifth birthday, I attended my very first wedding, for my friend Danielle. Claudio, Brian, Eric, and I were invited. Our inexperience showed right off the bat. Eric forgot his checkbook and put cash in the gift envelope instead. Claudio also forgot his checkbook so his dad had to write a check for him. After sadly discovering they don't make Snoopy cards for weddings, I mistakenly made out my check to Danielle's now-defunct maiden name. And Brian forgot a card altogether. But we all drank way too much to be embarrassed.

I THINK THERE should be a new reality show called *Who Wants to Try on My Tux?* Seriously, since I bought the thing for my freshman year fraternity formal, I must have had it taken in and out three times each. I'm afraid my tailor thinks I'm bulimic. Seven years later, though, I went into Danielle's wedding knowing it would be my tux's last stand. Held together by safety pins and sheer will, it emerged intact and I retired it to the back of my closet as yet another reminder of a winsome childhood giving way to a new and uncertain future. Or some bull-shit like that.

THE ACTUAL WEDDING was a blast. One of Danielle's college friends got so bombed, she passed out on the floor and had to be carried out of the party. At one point, as I was holding her up because she couldn't support her own weight, she actually tried to order another drink. I don't think I've ever seen a bartender laugh at someone like that before. Toward the end of the night, though, as we debated whether to call her a cab or an ambulance, one thought kept crossing my mind—thank God it's not me!

THE MOST ANNOYING part about the wedding was telling older people that it was my first one. Because they all had the same response: "Well, get ready, because you're gonna have one every weekend for the next five years! Lotta weddings, lotta money, get ready, soon everyone you know will be getting married!" I was like, chill out, I don't even know anyone else who is engaged!

WHILE MEETING GIRLFRIEND and going to my first wedding were huge steps for me, it's no big deal for others. Ironically enough, the day I was getting my tux taken out for Danielle's wedding, a friend forwarded me a porn site with what looked like another girl from my high school getting violated six ways to Sunday. It just goes to show the wide spectrum of the twentysomething mentality. Some of us are on our knees popping the question, while others of us are on our knees . . . OK, you see where I'm going with this one.

ALL OF A sudden, I absolutely hate getting mail. Remember back in the day how you never got mail and when you did it was usually something cool? Now that I'm getting older, everything in the mail is just bills, unsolicited credit card applications, and coupon books for goods and services I would never purchase. Nothing cool comes anymore except the occasional misaddressed Victoria's Secret catalog.

I'M NOT TOO worried about getting old, though. There are so many reasons why I still feel like a kid. For instance, whenever I find out that someone speaks a foreign language, I still ask them how to say "shit" and "fart." Most of the T-shirts I wear still say something to the effect of "Zeta Beta Tau Toga Party 2000." You can still see the piercing in my ear even though I haven't worn an earring in five years. The other day I got yelled at at the gym for throwing around one of those giant bouncy balls. Oh yeah, and I still went to a pediatrician until like last year. What? The nurses there are hot.

I'VE ALSO REALIZED that my perspective on growing older is definitely influenced by those younger than me. For instance, when I performed at a college in the midwest recently, it seemed like before the show everyone in the audience was a little, well, off. I pulled one of the girls aside and said, "Excuse me, um, are you . . . high?" And she said, "Yeah, we all are." "Why?" I asked. "Well," she said, "to see you." People were getting high just to see me! That's when you know you've made it.

I'VE FOUND THAT college kids assume that anyone who looks remotely like they are between sixteen and twenty-five years old is also in college. I was at Dartmouth for Caryn's graduation and her friend asked me what college I go to. I was like, "Well, actually I graduated three years ago." He was like "Oh, sorry to hear that." Like I died or something!

HERE'S HOW YOU can tell if someone is still in college or if they've graduated: whenever there's an empty space in a room or house, a college kid will always say, "Hey, let's put a bar there!"

AND HERE ARE two ways you can tell that you're getting old. When you have a party in your apartment, do you close the door of your bedroom so that no one goes in there? Also, have you started calling your friends by their first names when you've only called them by their last names for the past twenty years? If you answered yes to either of these questions, I recommend you see a pediatrician immediately!

JUST BEFORE MY twenty-fifth birthday, I was asked to come back to my old high school to speak to the graduating seniors. But I didn't want to be that guy at the assembly that no one is listening to, you know? What would I even tell the kids? That if they study hard, when they get to be my age they can still go on Spring Break, bang older chicks, become a lawyer or a doctor, create slang, get married, appear in online porn, or perform stand-up in front of hundreds of stoned sorority chicks? Hmm, now that I think about it, that'd be one pretty gourmet assembly . . .

IF I HAD spoken at the assembly, I'd probably tell the seniors that it bothers me that only Oscar winners and championship athletes say, "If you follow your dreams and don't give up, you will succeed." Of course you're saying that, you just won the fucking Stanley Cup! You never see any homeless people saying not to give up.

WHEN THE BIG birthday finally arrived, I decided to celebrate the end of my early twenties in style. Instead of inviting all my friends to a stupid club that no one would be able to get into anyway, I organized a mid-afternoon pub crawl up Third Avenue. Everyone received a souvenir cup and a map of the festivities. At each bar, I was joined by more and more of my twentysomething companions—Girlfriend, Brian, high school friends, fraternity buddies, former co-workers, even Danielle called in from her honeymoon. As we crawled on, the bars began to run together, my words slurred, and the clock ticked closer to midnight. And before I knew it, it was all over, and I was a twenty-five-year-old man. Eating birthday cake without utensils and covered head to toe in beer. But twenty-five nonetheless.

THE NEXT DAY, I was suffering from a severe case of post-party depression. I was hungover. My early twenties were over. And I couldn't get the chocolate cake out from behind my ears. I decided to go to the movies to cheer up, but had to go by myself because all my friends had already gone without me. Now I was old and not very cool either. As the previews began, a couple of junior high kids whose parents were clearly not with them came down the aisle and tapped me on the shoulder. Good, I thought to myself, I can't be that old and uncool if these guys still think I'm approachable. I thought wrong. "Excuse me, sir," the first kid said. "This movie is rated R and we snuck in. Since you're alone, if the usher comes by, will you say you're our dad?" Fuck me!

AFTERWORD
is there life after twentysomething?

Looking back upon my Whatever Years, I think that I spent a lot of time feeling uneasy. I constantly had that feeling of dread that someone who didn't deserve it was going to strike it big before I did. It's the same feeling you get when you're watching your dumbest, laziest, most dim-witted friend play the lottery. You're sort of rooting for him, but deep down you're thinking, if this idiot wins a million bucks a week for life I'm just going to shoot myself. Now I know that wasn't how I should feel. Because no matter how many dues you pay, in the lottery of twentysomething life, there's always going to be some moron who wins first. But that doesn't mean you can't have fun playing along.

One thing that I've learned since I turned twenty-five is that things only change as much as you allow them to. Brian may have long since moved out of our apartment and in with his girlfriend, but that doesn't stop me from harassing him via email on a daily basis. Caryn may have moved to that godforsaken place called Los Angeles, but that doesn't mean our names rhyme any less annoyingly. And though I'm now closer to thirty years old than I am to twenty, the bar is still the same distance away. In other words, the end of your Whatever Years is not the end of the world. You can always reminisce about the crazy times you had, assuming there's anything you can actually remember.

But it is time to look ahead. I've set some pretty lofty goals for my late twenties. I have dreams. I'd like to win an Emmy. I'd also like to appear in a music video surrounded by brunettes in wife-beaters with the logo on my T-shirt inexplicably blurred out. But there's really one thing that I want more than anything else—my own toilet. Now, I'm not talking about having my own bathroom, plenty of people my age have that. But others can use it. I'm talking about a toilet that I and only I am ever allowed to use. One whose lid answers only to me. That's right, a virgin bowl. It may seem silly to some, but to me, having a virgin bowl marks true success in this world. It means wealth, power, and cleanliness. But I digress. The fact of the matter is that, yes, I believe there is life after twentysomething, and it's limited only by what you can imagine. And hey, I made it all the way to the second to last paragraph of this book without getting cheesy on you.

In the end, I think that our early twenties are marked by size, or rather lack thereof. We are trapped in tiny cubicles and living in cramped apartments, earning minuscule salaries and getting laid way too little. But we still dream big. With that in mind, try not to let the inevitable setbacks of twentysomething life get you down. And when shit hits the fan and everyone is looking to you for answers you don't have, I hope you'll think of me and, with a glint in your eye, shrug your shoulders and say, "Fuck me."

—Karo
March 2005
New York City